AN IDIOT'S G
TO THE BOOK OI

GW01035565

Joanne D Cameron

AN IDIOT'S GUIDE TO THE BOOK OF DANIEL

Joanne D Cameron

First published in 2020 by KAD Publishing

240 Bounces Road, London N9 8LA

Copyright © 2020 Joanne D Cameron

All rights reserved. No part of this book may be reproduced in any manner whatsoever or stored in any information storage system, without the prior written consent of the publisher or the author, except in the case of brief quotations with proper reference, embodied in critical articles and reviews. All quotations remain the intellectual property of the originator. All use of quotations is done under the fair use copyright principle.

Record of this book is available from the British Library.

An Idiot's Guide to the Book of Daniel

Joanne D Cameron

Cover design by Sharon Thornhill

ISBN 978-1-9160249-6-0

Dedicated to Anthony
My partner three times over

Table of Contents

Illustrations

Acknowledgements

As the Author of this book, I must admit it was not a lone project. Were it not for the help, support and influence of others, this work would never have been accomplished. And I am therefore extremely grateful to the following individuals. I would like to thank Dr Keith Davidson for helping me believe I was capable of writing this book. Without his encouragement I would not have even contemplated embarking on the project.

I would also like to acknowledge the following family members. My sister Claudia Crawley, an Author in her own right. As my older sister, she has always been my trailblazer.

My daughter Kelly Aliowe, and her husband, Olawale Aliowe, who read my first drafts and enthusiastically advised me to continue.

Thanks also to my younger daughter, Sophie Holder, who loves to tell the absolute truth as she sees it and is therefore an expert constructive critic.

My Bible Study group have also been excellent supporters. They have shown such interest in this work; not only assuring their own readiness to read it, but also their willingness to engage in activities to disseminate it abroad.

My friend, Mervyn Weir, was also very helpful in reading the draft, and giving much needed marketing advice.

And, of course, I must acknowledge the artists, Guy Chapman and Gilda Melisa Castagnone who provided the illustrations. Guy is a sincere Christian, and we became great friends during this project. I have loved working with him, and his drawings are unique, breath taking, and certainly a talking point for everyone who views them. The more you look at them the more you see; their subtle details are truly amazing. Particularly, I would like to thank Gilda who stepped in at the eleventh hour to complete the book's illustrations, and was an absolute joy to work with. I will certainly be working with her on future projects. I feel very fortunate to have met and worked with these two accomplished artists.

I must also thank KAD Publishing for its editorial hints and its agreement to publish this work.

And last, but certainly not least, I would like to thank Anthony Lloyd Cameron, my husband. Without his tireless support, and love, this book would never have been written. He believed in me when I did not believe in myself. Anthony has read, re-read and edited this book many times. His attention to detail has been exemplary.

Of course, God has been the driving force behind it all. He gave me the idea to write the book, which is no more than a poor woman's explanation of His text – the book of Daniel as found in the Holy Bible, God inspired me to write, and was with me every step of the way in interpreting His holy words. It is my prayer this work will bring glory to His name.

Joanne D Cameron

Foreword

Dear Reader,

Thank you for opening this book.

I hope you find it stimulating and meaningful.

My reason for writing it was, firstly, because I have heard so many people say the Bible's prophetic books are mysteries that cannot be understood. Or, the fulfilment of the prophecies are set so far in our future they have no relevance for us. Both these assertions are simply not true. The book of Daniel was given to mankind specifically for our time. Much of its prophecies have already been fulfilled, and are therefore historically verifiable. The only predictions left to take place are the end time events that will usher in the coming of Jesus. Therefore, it is imperative that every person on planet earth understand its message.

Secondly, there are quite a few books available that aim to explain the book of Daniel. However, apart from the fact that most of them are as heavy as doorstops, and therefore difficult to read as normal books while you are commuting, or sitting in your local coffee shop, they also appear to be written for intellectuals, and not for the average woman/man in the street.

Thirdly, the books already available do not appear to be concerned with Daniel himself, but only with the prophecies contained in his book. My reading of the book of Daniel impresses me that this is a book about Daniel the man. He was seventeen years old at the beginning of the book and 89 at the close. This is a book about a man's life; all that he experienced through his long and extraordinary lifetime. It is Daniel's story.

This book was written to provide a good read for any ordinary person interested in Daniel, the man, and the prophecies he was given by God for the people of our time. The fact that the prophecies have been fulfilled to the letter throughout Daniel's time, have continued to be fulfilled down through the ages, thousands of years after they were given to Daniel, and are still being fulfilled today, are a sure testimony to the reliability and credibility of the Bible, and provide undeniable evidence that the prophecies, soon to be fulfilled in our future, will take place just as predicted.

Ladies, you can slip this book in your handbag. Gents, you can pop it into your briefcase (or man bag). You can read it on the train, in the office, the park or wherever you choose. And, at a hundred and fifty pages, or so, it is an easy read, written in plain English with no long words to decipher.

My main source, of course, is the book of Daniel itself. I have included other biblical references, where appropriate. I have mainly used the New International Version (NIV), unless indicated otherwise. If you do not want to look up the references as you read, you don't need to; they have been included to let you know where we are in Daniel, and provide evidence of what has been written. Other references are labelled in the text and listed at the back of the book. You will notice some historical information used come from websites. These have been included to show the availability of historical facts to us all. I hope these references do not lessen your belief in the seriousness of this book.

I specifically want to thank the book's illustrators, Guy Chapman and Gilda Melisa Castagnone. I hope the wonderful illustrations enhance your reading and help you grasp the many vivid images that make up Daniel's dreams and visions.

If you are wondering why the book is called 'An Idiot's Guide to the Book of Daniel'? I just wanted to let readers know the book of Daniel is for everyone. We can all understand it. I hope no-one is offended by the title.

You may be interested to learn that this book is a companion to another of my works on Bible prophecy called 'An Idiot's Guide to the Book of Revelation'. If you appreciate this publication, you might be interested in reading its companion, which takes a step-by-step journey through the Bible's book of Revelation.

I hope you enjoy this book.

Joanne D Cameron

Daniel Chapter One

BEING A CHRISTIAN MEANS BEING A HERO EVERY DAY OF YOUR LIFE

Based on Daniel 1:1-21

Our story begins with a sad episode in Jewish history called the Babylonian Captivity. From 605BC – 539BC the ancient kingdom of Babylon ruled the then known world. Soon after coming to power, Babylon turned its attention to the southern Jewish kingdom, Judah, and its capital city, Jerusalem. And, for a period of nearly 20 years, laid siege after protracted siege against the city, until finally destroying both Jerusalem and its temple in 587BC.

Daniel 1:1 - tells the story in a nutshell. It simply says *"In the third year of the reign of Jehoiakim, king of Judah, Nebuchadnezzar, king of Babylon, came to Jerusalem and besieged it."*

Daniel 1:2 – reveals it was God's plan for the Jews, His chosen people, to suffer defeat. He delivered king Jehoiakim into King Nebuchadnezzar's hand. In addition, He allowed the heathen Babylonians to confiscate holy articles from the Jewish temple. The articles made of silver and gold were placed in the Babylonian temple, and the treasure house of their idol god, Marduk. Not only was the Jewish nation defeated, it was utterly disgraced.

The Bible has always portrayed Jerusalem as the city of God; it is the place where God's temple was situated, and where His people assembled to worship Him. Jerusalem means 'city of peace'. Babylon, on the other hand, is portrayed as the place where the wicked dwell. It seems incomprehensible that God would engineer the conquest of His own people at the hands of blatant idol worshipers.

Here is a tale of two cities. Jerusalem versus Babylon; good versus evil. Careful contrast of these two cities gives insight into the age old controversy between good and evil. Genesis 11:1-9 is the first Biblical reference to Babel where the infamous Tower was built, and from where ancient Babylon took its name. The Tower of Babel was where God confused the speech of the builders, causing them to separate and leave the tower's construction unfinished. Babel (or Babylon) means confusion. The Babylonians, as idol worshipers, were enemies of the true God. Then, in Revelation 14:8 and 17:5, we are introduced to *"Babylon the Great"*, the symbol of the apostate church through all ages, whose false doctrines cause confusion and lack of spiritual clarity. Babylon the Great is the power that persecutes and oppresses God's people. It is controlled by the devil himself. From the first to the last books of the Bible we find Babylon, symbol of the kingdom of the devil.

In Revelation 21, the New Jerusalem is described as the heavenly city built by God, where He will dwell throughout eternity with His people on the earth made new. Despite all the evil inspired work of the devil, Revelation 21 confirms that good will triumph over evil; the city of God conquers the city of Babylon.

In Daniel chapter one we see both ancient Jerusalem, signifying God's dwelling with His people, and Babylon, signifying the kingdom of the devil. Here, evil has triumphed. Why would God allow this to happen?

The answer lies in the behaviour of God's people (see 2 Kings 21:10-16, 2 Kings 24:18-20, 2 Chronicles 36:15-19, Jeremiah 3:13). These texts paint a disturbing picture of the continual evil perpetrated by the kings of the Jewish nation. One after another, these kings shed innocent blood, led the nation into the worship of idols, disregarded the poor and needy, and committed every type of detestable practice imaginable.

God's people were warned (see Jeremiah 4:1-4). They were given ample time to change their appalling ways and return to God, but they refused, and the judgements of the Lord were meted out. In other words, God withdrew His protection from His people, and Babylon was allowed to conquer them.

The Old Testament books of Kings and Chronicles catalogue the misbehaviour of the Jewish nation, which seemed incapable of remaining faithful to its God. When led by a god-fearing king, the nation became god-fearing, but more often, its kings rejected the law of God and led their people into following the practices of their idolatrous neighbours. No wonder God finally allowed the nation to suffer the consequences of its wayward actions.

Daniel 1:3-4 – In our story, king Nebuchadnezzar transports to Babylon, prisoners of war from Judah's royal family and nobility. Ashpenaz, chief of the king's court officials, is instructed to bring young, handsome, men only, with no physical defects, who are intelligent and have an aptitude for learning. These prisoners are to be taught the language of their captors, and study Babylonian literature.

Daniel 1:5 – Although prisoners of war, these young men are being highly favoured, for they are assigned a daily portion of food and wine from the king's table. They will be trained for three years, and then enter the king's service. Nebuchadnezzar is investing a great deal in these prisoners. No doubt, a great deal will be expected of them.

Daniel 1:6 - Among those selected are Daniel, Hananiah, Mishael and Azariah; young men, physically fit, handsome and intelligent, soon to embark on their adult lives. Daniel is 17 years old.

Each of these young men fulfil all the necessary criteria, and in addition, they are followers of Jehovah. As we shall see, their faith becomes paramount in influencing their conduct in this very strange, and no doubt frightening, situation.

They were teenagers, kept alive because of their youth and appearance. The majority of Jews had been killed. Therefore, these young men were mourning

3

the loss of family members and friends, possibly killed in front of them. They had lost their homes, their possessions, everything familiar; carried far from Jerusalem by their conquerors to an uncertain future, at the mercy of these ungodly enemies. In the King James Version of the Bible, we are told that Ashpenaz was not only the chief of court officials, but the master of eunuchs (Daniel 1:3). It appears, therefore, that Daniel, Hananiah, Mishael and Azariah were castrated as part of their preparation for servitude. The temptation to believe that God had abandoned them must have been overwhelming.

Daniel 1:7 – In an effort to strip them of their Jewish identity, the youths are given new names, signifying allegiance to Babylonian deity. Daniel is named Belteshazzar; Hananiah is called Shadrach; Mishael is renamed Meshach; and Azariah becomes Abednego.

As this is the book of Daniel, we will continue to refer to him by his Jewish name.

Daniel 1:8 – When faced with the prospect of eating unclean food, albeit from the king's table, the 17 year old Daniel makes a decision. As a Jew, Daniel obeys the law given to Moses by God on Mount Sinai. Of course, the most important of these was the Ten Commandments (see Exodus 20:3-17). But also included in God's requirements were the health laws (see Leviticus 11) forbidding the eating of animals, birds, fish or insects, not created for food. Daniel knows that unclean meat is included in the Babylonian diet, and is determined to obey God. He is fully aware that to defy the king will almost certainly lead to his demise. He is a prisoner of war, with no rights, no status and no legal precedents. However, Daniel believes God will reward his endeavour to be faithful. There is no doubt, the king's food would also be dedicated to Marduk, the idol god, before being consumed. Therefore, to eat it would show allegiance to the pagan god. Daniel decides to be a hero for Jehovah. He calls Ashpenaz aside and asks for permission to be excused from eating the king's food.

Being a Christian requires heroism every day of your life. Followers of Christ need to purpose in their hearts each day not to defile themselves with practices out of harmony with the will of God, just as Daniel did. Situations will occur that call for compromise and compliance, but the child of God will determine that he (or she) must obey God rather than man (Acts 5:29). The opportunities to be a hero for God may be small, and undetectable to others. They may involve your behaviour in the workplace, how you conduct your daily tasks, how you speak to, and interact with others, or what you eat (like Daniel). Whatever the situation, or whatever the consequence, it is good to remember that God is alert to all our actions, and decisions, and every circumstance is an opportunity to step out and be a hero for Him.

Some might consider it prudent for Daniel and his friends to submit at this point, for by not complying with the king's command, they were putting their lives on the line. Nebuchadnezzar would not have thought twice about having them executed for refusing his gracious offer. Therefore, the Hebrew teenagers could have rationalised that to eat the king's food would be a minor misdemeanour. They could have reasoned that it would be unlikely for God to preserve their lives during the destruction of Jerusalem, only to see them killed over food. As tempting as this reasoning may have been, the boys remained faithful to the law of Moses; they were prepared to die rather than disobey God. It is clear Daniel had already resolved that God's will would take priority in his life. When it came to making a decision to either save his life, or serve God, he chose to serve God. What a lesson for us. (See Matt 10:22, Philippians 3:8, 2 Tim 2:12).

Daniel 1:9 – tells us, God had already caused Ashpenaz to be favourably disposed towards Daniel. Perhaps Ashpenaz saw something different in the four Hebrew boys. There was something about the way they conducted themselves, that he liked. Therefore, when Daniel approaches him with a very dangerous request, he does not throw it out, but reasons with Daniel, and lets him know his thoughts.

It is reassuring to consider that whilst we may worry about the consequences of stepping out as a hero for God, He knows what we intend to do, and prepares the way for us, even causing people with influence to act on our behalf. God never leaves His children isolated; He involves Himself in their actions and smooths the way for those who seek to do His will (see Matthew 10:32).

Daniel 1:10 – Ashpenaz confides in Daniel that he fears to grant his request; for surely this will lead to the four friends looking less healthy than the rest of the trainees. Ashpenaz is afraid that, should this happen, the king will have him executed for failing to take care of the young men under his supervision.

Daniel 1:11-13 – Daniel then has an idea. He asks Ashpenaz to conduct an experiment by giving the four of them nothing but vegetables to eat and water to drink. Then, at the end of ten days compare them with the rest of the young men. After that, Ashpenaz can decide how to proceed.

Daniel 1:14 – Ashpenaz agrees to carry out the experiment.

Daniel 1:15-16 – At the end of ten days, the Hebrew boys look healthier and better nourished than all the other trainees eating the king's food. So, Ashpenaz puts them all on a diet of vegetables and water.

Just a word here about diet. When God created the world and put Adam and Eve in the garden, He gave them instructions regarding what they should eat. Genesis 1:29 tells us their diet was *"seed bearing plants and fruit from trees that bear seeds",* in other words a vegan diet. Eating meat was not originally intended for mankind. Therefore, the human body will always thrive, and become healthy, on a plant based diet with plenty of water. The experience of the four Hebrew boys proves this.

Daniel 1:17 – God blesses Daniel, Shadrach, Meshach and Abednego during the three years of training by giving them heightened knowledge and understanding in all kinds of literature and learning. Moreover, Daniel gains the spiritual gift of being able to understand and interpret dreams and visions. This skill is going to prove very useful to Daniel as we progress through his book.

Here is a note for students of all ages. If you want to excel in your study programme, eat and drink healthily, exercise daily, and ask God to open your understanding and capacity to learn. He who created man's intellect is certainly able to heighten your ability to use that intellect to learn, retain, revise and regurgitate.

Daniel 1:18-20 – At the end of the three years of training, all the trainees are presented to king Nebuchadnezzar for scrutiny. The king examines each one, and finds Daniel, Shadrach, Meshach and Abednego are not only the most accomplished of all the trainees, but because of their superior wisdom and understanding, the answers they give to all his questions are ten times better than those of his existing magicians and enchanters throughout the entire kingdom. The four young men are engaged in the king's service.

Daniel 1:21 – This verse gives a footnote. We are told Daniel remained in his role of advisor to foreign kings until the first year of king Cyrus. We will come across Daniel's time with Cyrus. He was nearly 90 years old when he served this Persian king.

Daniel chapter one is an introduction that aptly sets the scene for the actions and adventures to come. We will learn that even as a prisoner of war, a Christian, determined to follow godly principles, whatever the circumstance, will excel. The four Hebrew boys were trailblazers. They put God first in everything, and trusted in His guidance and protection. They did not fear the mightiest of kings, for their King was the Creator of the universe. And, because of their trust in Him, God equipped them to be extraordinary in His service.

The book of Daniel contains spectacular dreams and visions, with prophetic messages for our time. We will also encounter angel interpreters, supernatural experiences, and even a werewolf. At the middle of it all, is the life of Daniel, a true hero for God.

Daniel Chapter Two

"TELL ME THE DREAM, OR ELSE!"

Based on Daniel 2:1-49

Daniel 2:1 – In the second year of his reign, Nebuchadnezzar, king of Babylon, has a dream. He wakes up startled and troubled, and lays awake for the rest of the night. He knows the dream is important. Apparently, the Babylonians believed all dreams were significant. For this reason Nebuchadnezzar's court was filled with magicians, enchanters, sorcerers and astrologers. The Babylonians were fiercely superstitious.

Daniel 2:2-3 - Nebuchadnezzar summons his soothsayers and tells them he has had a disturbing dream and needs it to be interpreted.

Daniel 2:4 – This was not an uncommon occurrence for the royal soothsayers. They were used to giving interpretations to the king's dreams. They ask the king to tell them what he has dreamed.

Daniel 2:5 - However, the king is no fool. Perhaps his magicians, enchanters, sorcerers and astrologers have given suspect interpretations to previous dreams. This dream is too important, and so the king decides to do something different. He will not reveal the details of the dream. For, after all, if they are authentic wise men, conversant with the magic arts, they will be able to consult the spirits and tell him his dream. Nebuchadnezzar informs them that if they cannot tell him what he has dreamed, and give the dream's meaning, by royal decree, they will be cut into pieces and their houses completely destroyed. All of a sudden, what was first a common occurrence is now a life and death situation.

Daniel 2:6 – The king adds that if they are able to tell the dream and its meaning, all will be well. They will receive gifts, rewards, and great honour. This is no consolation to the wise men, as clearly, they cannot tell the king his dream.

Daniel 2:7 – The soothsayers desperately play for time. They try to persuade the king to do as he has always done; tell them his dream. Then they will be only too pleased to give an explanation.

Daniel 2:8-9 – But the king is not for turning. He realises they are stalling and once again repeats, if they do not carry out his request they will suffer the penalty. He knows that in the past they have conspired to give him wicked and misleading advice, and they intend to do so now. The time has come for them to prove they can do what they say they can do. If they can correctly tell him his dream, then he will know they are real magicians.

Daniel 2:10-11 – The game is up. The soothsayers finally admit the king's request is beyond their capability. They complain that he is being unreasonable, as no human being can do what he asks. Moreover, no king, however great and mighty, has ever asked any magician, enchanter, or astrologer to do anything like this. They are peeved. They say, no-one but the gods, who do not live amongst men, can reveal the dream to Nebuchadnezzar. In their frustration, the soothsayers expose themselves as imposters. All their previous advice to the king is proved worthless. They have known all along that the supernatural powers they claim to possess, belong only to God.

Daniel 2:12-15 - The king is furious. The admission of the wise men confirms his suspicions, but does not solve his problem. In a rage, he orders the death of all the wise men in Babylon, including Daniel, Shadrach, Meshach and Abednego.

Arioch, the king's officer, arrives at Daniel's house to carry out the death decree. Daniel has no idea what is going on, and so tactfully asks Arioch to explain why he is to be put to death. Arioch explains the whole matter.

Daniel 2:16 – Daniel then does something very bold. He goes to see the king, and asks for time to interpret the dream. The king is angry and frustrated, but agrees to Daniel's request. This shows the character of Daniel. He is dealing with a king in a fit of rage. Nebuchadnezzar has been let down by all his wise men. Yet Daniel, a young and inexperienced member of court, a Jew, under the threat of death, is able to calmly approach the king and ask for time. Daniel's bravery is magnificent, but so is his faith; for he believes, beyond a shadow of doubt, God will reveal the dream to him.

Daniel 2:17-19 - Daniel calls his three friends and explains everything to them. They then hold a prayer meeting, and sure enough, during the night, their faith is rewarded. God reveals to Daniel a vision of the king's dream. And the first thing Daniel does is praise God.

Daniel 2:20-23 - Here is Daniel's song of praise:

> *"Praise be to the name of God for ever and ever;*
> *wisdom and power are His.*
> *He changes times and seasons;*
> *He deposes kings and raises up others.*
> *He gives wisdom to the wise*
> *and knowledge to the discerning.*
> *He reveals deep and hidden things;*
> *He knows what lies in darkness,*
> *and light dwells with Him.*
> *I thank and praise you, God of my ancestors:*
> *You have given me wisdom and power,*
> *You have made known to us the dream of the king."*

Daniel's song gives us insight into Nebuchadnezzar's dream, for as we will learn, it concerns the raising and deposing of kings. And, we can now understand why the king was so perturbed. His dream was an answer from God, as he pondered during the night regarding the longevity of his kingdom.

Daniel 2:24 – Daniel quickly goes to Arioch and tells him to stay the execution of the wise men. Instead, he asks Arioch to take him to the king so that he can reveal the dream and its interpretation.

Daniel 2:25-26 – Arioch announces to the king that Daniel is able to interpret his dream, and Nebuchadnezzar excitedly asks Daniel if this is true.

Daniel 2:27-28 – Of course, the answer to the king's question is 'yes'. Daniel is the only one of the wise men able to fulfil his request. But, surprisingly Daniel answers 'no'. He says *"No wise man, enchanter, magician or diviner can explain to the king the mystery he has asked about."*

You can imagine the disappointment, and confusion, registered on Nebuchadnezzar's face. What is Daniel up to? He knows what the dream is. Why would he answer the king in this way? Daniel is making a point, which we should all remember. The admission of the wise men is indeed true. To be able to know the details of another person's dream (without them telling you) is not a skill human beings possess. Daniel is being very careful to make Nebuchadnezzar understand that all he is about to reveal was given to him by God. Daniel will not take credit for what he is about to disclose.

Daniel tells the king *"..there is a God in heaven who reveals mysteries. He has shown king Nebuchadnezzar what will happen in days to come. Your dream and the visions that passed through your mind as you were lying in bed are these.."*

Daniel 2:29-30 – Daniel was not only shown Nebuchadnezzar's dream, he also saw the king before he fell asleep. He viewed him lying on his bed turning over in his mind thoughts about the future of his kingdom. The dream is God's response to Nebuchadnezzar's brooding.

Daniel makes it clear that God did not reveal the mystery to him because he is wiser than anyone else, but so the king might get the understanding of his dream, which answers the questions troubling his mind.

So now we are clear, the dream was given to Nebuchadnezzar by God, and concerns kings and kingdoms to come.

Daniel 2:31–35 – King Nebuchadnezzar's dream:
The king dreamed of an enormous, dazzling statue. Its head was made of gold, its chest and arms were silver, its belly and thighs were of bronze, its legs were made of iron, and the feet were a mixture of iron and clay. A rock which was supernaturally hewn, hit the statue at its feet and smashed them. Then the clay, iron, bronze, silver and gold were broken in pieces, and became like dust swept away by the wind, leaving nothing. The rock, however, became a huge mountain that filled the whole earth.

Daniel 2:36-45 – The king is elated. Daniel has reported the dream in every minute detail. He now eagerly awaits the interpretation.

Daniel begins the explanation respectfully with *"Your Majesty, you are the king of kings. The God of heaven has given you dominion and power and might and glory. In your hands He has placed all mankind and the beasts of the field and the birds in the sky. Wherever they live, He has made you ruler over them all. You are that head of gold."* The golden head of the statue represents the kingdom of Babylon.

All this was true. Nebuchadnezzar was the ruler of the greatest power on earth. Babylon was the first world ruling empire. There was no-one greater than he. In addition, Daniel tactfully informs the king that everything he has achieved was granted to him by God. Nevertheless, Daniel's words must have painted a huge smile on Nebuchadnezzar's face: God was acknowledging him as the greatest king on earth.

However, here follows some not so good news. The kingdom of Babylon will not rule forever. It will be overthrown by an inferior, or less wealthy, kingdom, as signified by the statue's chest and arms of silver. History tells us the joint kingdom of the Medes and Persians (Medo-Persia) overthrew Babylon in 539BC.

The statue's belly and thighs of bronze represented the kingdom of Greece, which in 331BC conquered the Persian Empire, and ruled the then known world until it too was overtaken by the kingdom of Rome in 168BC. This fourth world ruling kingdom, represented by the statue's legs of iron, is described as being as strong as iron; smashing and breaking everything in its path.

Then in AD476, the Roman Empire would be replaced by a divided kingdom represented by the feet and ten toes of the statue made partly of iron and partly of clay. Just as iron is strong and clay is malleable, the divided kingdom would be made up of both powerful and weak nations. These nations would be continually attempting to unite into one kingdom, but would never achieve it.

It is interesting to note that each successive kingdom is represented by a metal inferior to the one before it. Babylon was indeed a golden kingdom, sumptuous and opulent in its lifestyle, its structures, and its natural features. The hanging gardens of Babylon were one of the seven wonders of the ancient world. The kingdom that conquered Babylon (Medo-Persia) was less affluent, less luxuriant, in fact, inferior in every way. Yet it overthrew the great kingdom. Greece, led by Alexander the Great, a brilliant, power-hungry young man, owned less riches and resources than Medo-Persia, and thus is represented by bronze. Then Rome is portrayed as iron, a non-precious metal. It is clear Rome's power lay not in its wealth but in its military strength and ability to demolish all surrounding nations. We will come across these empires again. The divided kingdom is a mixture of the strength of iron and the weak pliability of common clay. Surely an indication of this kingdom's character and financial status.

Humanity flatters itself that each successive generation is superior to its predecessor. Moreover, that with the increase in knowledge and technology, we are continually evolving and progressing towards utopia. However, the statue in Nebuchadnezzar's dream appears to indicate the opposite. As the world's empires deteriorate, so do its societies, until we reach a situation of vacillating government, with grandiose ideas of unity they cannot realise. This will be the state of affairs when Jesus returns.

We can give no end date for the divided kingdom because it will remain divided until the Second Advent, signified by the rock, cut out by non-human hands. It strikes the statue at its feet showing that Jesus' coming will take place in the time of the divided kingdom. It brings the statue toppling down and smashes it into dust, which is blown away. Then the rock grows and fills the whole earth. The dream makes it clear the second coming of Jesus will destroy all earthly kingdoms, and God will set up His kingdom on the earth to rule forever.

Here is a table of the world ruling empires:

Empire:	Dates:
Babylon	605BC – 539BC
Medo-Persia	539BC – 331BC
Greece	331BC – 168BC
Rome	168BC – AD476
Divided Kingdom	AD476 – Second Advent
Kingdom of God	Second Advent - Eternity

The dream's earthly empires covered the then known world encompassing the general area of Europe, and including Britain to the north, northern Africa to the south and even parts of India. AD476 saw the Roman Empire separated into ten kingdoms, which loosely make up today's European Union.

Daniel concludes the interpretation by reminding the king that it is God who has shown him the future, and therefore the dream is true, and its interpretation trustworthy.

Daniel 2:46-49 – Nebuchadnezzar is overwhelmed by what he has heard. He falls prostrate before Daniel, and attempts to confer divine status on him by ordering that he be presented with incense and offerings. Daniel is promoted to become the ruler of the entire Babylonian province. He is showered with gifts, and put in charge of all the wise men at court. At Daniel's request, Shadrach, Meshach and Abednego are appointed administrators over the province of Babylon.

The experience also leads the king to praise the God of heaven. He says to Daniel *"Surely your God is the God of gods and the Lord of kings and a revealer of mysteries, for you were able to reveal this mystery."* We cannot say the king has become a convert, at this stage, but at least he is able to acknowledge there is something very powerful about Daniel's God.

King Nebuchadnezzar received his dream over 2,500 years ago. To him it was prophecy. To us it is history, and has been fulfilled to the letter, which is compelling evidence of the authenticity of the Bible. As Daniel confirms: the Bible has been given by God; it is true and trustworthy.

One section of the dream is still to be fulfilled, and as every predicted event has happened so far, there is no reason to believe the remaining features will not also take place exactly as stated. We are presently living in the time of the toes of iron mixed with clay. The nations of Europe are indeed divided. Since the fall of the Roman Empire, attempts have been made to unite Europe under one leader, such as, Charlemagne (AD800-AD814), the Holy Roman Empire (AD800-1806), Napoleon (1799-1815), and Hitler (1939-1945). All have failed, just as prophesied. The dream predicts that attempts at unification will continue until Jesus comes. The European Union, first instituted in 1951, is surely the latest attempt. However, the 2016 British referendum, to decide whether the United Kingdom should remain in the European Union, is a testament to the veracity of king Nebuchadnezzar's dream. Despite all expectations to the contrary, the British public voted to leave the Union (Brexit); further proof that Bible prophecy can be trusted.

According to Nebuchadnezzar's dream, we are living in the closing period of earth's history, Jesus is soon to come.

Daniel Chapter Three

"EVEN IF HE DOESN'T"

Based on Daniel 3:1-30

At the end of Daniel chapter two we saw Nebuchadnezzar, ruler of the greatest kingdom in the world, lying prostrate before Daniel, a young Jewish prisoner of war. The king has been brought to his knees, for he realises Daniel serves a mighty God, who reveals the future to His servants. Despite this touching scene, let us not forget that Nebuchadnezzar has received some disturbing news; his kingdom will not last forever. He must have wondered whether there was something he could do to prevent the prophecy's fulfilment.

Daniel 3:1 – Nebuchadnezzar decides to amend the details of his God-given dream. In the dream he saw a great statue made of diverse metals, signifying the world ruling empires leading up to the Second Advent. The king's response is to build a great statue of his own, ninety feet high by nine feet wide. He orders that the statue be situated in the spacious plain of Dura. There is one major difference between his statue and the statue in his dream; his statue is made entirely of one metal – gold. Clearly, Nebuchadnezzar was proclaiming a prophecy of his own - the Babylonian Empire will never be defeated.

Daniel 3:2-3 – The king summons all the government officials to the statue's dedication ceremony (satraps, prefects, governors, advisors, treasurers, judges, magistrates, provincial officials). All the important people are there.

Daniel 3:4-6 - The decree is given. The royal orchestra is present, and as soon as the music plays, this is the cue for all in attendance to bow to the magnificent statue. Anyone refusing to bow will be immediately thrown into a blazing furnace. Because his subjects originate from different nations, with many languages, the king uses music to galvanize the people to action.

Music has always been a universal language. It transcends national and cultural barriers. Because of this, the modern music industry is a global enterprise. A song composed in one country can quickly become a hit in every country of the world, generating multi-millions of pounds in revenue. Music is also an influencer; it enters the brain without filters. It needs no translation. Through today's media, It can reach everyone, everywhere, and there is no age limit for those affected by it. There are so many songs in the Bible, it is clear God created music to enhance the worship experience of His created beings. Music is therefore a blessing to humanity. There is even evidence that God Himself sings (see Zephaniah 3:17). And, in the book of Revelation we see many instances of beings in heaven singing songs of praise before the throne of God (see Revelation 5:8-10, 15:3,4). However, the purpose for which music was created can be abused. Increasingly, music is used to perpetrate evil.

The devil is familiar with music. Ezekiel 28:13 (KJV) describes the anatomy of the magnificent angel, Lucifer, who later became the devil:
"Thou hast been in Eden the garden of God; every precious stone was thy covering, the sardius, topaz, and the diamond, the beryl, the onyx, and the jasper, the sapphire, the emerald, and the carbuncle, and gold: the workmanship of thy tabrets [tambourines] *and of thy pipes was prepared in thee in the day that thou wast created."*

The above quotation tells us that as well as being covered with precious stones, musical instruments were built within Lucifer's physical anatomy. Therefore, it appears that when he walked he made music. The devil is a music expert. He knows the powerful effect it has on human beings. He will therefore cause music to be used as a medium to entice people into evil. King Nebuchadnezzar used music to influence people of all nations to defy God.

22

Daniel 3:7 - The orchestra begins to play and the multitude of people do as they have been commanded; they all bow down to the golden statue, all that is, except three.

Daniel 3:8-12 – A report from some of the astrologers reaches the king. Remember, the astrologers have been humiliated by Daniel, who was able to reveal the king's dream, when they could not. And Daniel, a Jew, has been made their manager. They are obviously seeking revenge against the four Hebrew boys. They now report to the king that despite the music being played, there are three people standing upright. Shadrach, Meshach and Abednego are publically demonstrating their refusal to worship, or bow before, any god other than Jehovah.

From Daniel chapter one, we know the Hebrew boys have determined in their minds to only obey the God of heaven. The first two of the Ten Commandments forbid the worship of other gods, and the bowing to idols (see Exodus 20:3-6). Therefore, despite the threat of death, the boys had no choice; they must stand erect.

We are not told where Daniel is at this time. Perhaps he was away on official business, but from his previous actions it is certain that, had he been present, he would have joined his three friends in their protest. Shadrach, Meshach and Abednego are not swayed by the beautiful melody. They understand this situation is all about worship.

When people make a stand for God someone will always notice. The Christian life is not for people wishing to remain anonymous, nor for those who seek to melt into the background. Christians are required to be different, and to stand out (see 1 Peter 2:9 [KJV]). People who adopt godly principles in our society will attract attention. They will appear odd and strange to their peers, but they must continue to act in line with God's requirements, for He has called them to show forth His character to the world.

As with their experience regarding eating food from the king's table, Shadrach, Meshach and Abednego could certainly have given rational reasons for complying with the king's order. A man made golden statue could not be mistaken for the true and living God. So, perhaps they could have bowed down, but remain true to God in their hearts. Shadrach, Meshach and Abednego decided to obey the Ten Commandments.

Some religions, such as Catholicism, Hinduism and Buddhism teach the bowing, or praying, to statues as part of their religious practice. This is forbidden by the Bible. God created us to worship Him. Therefore, even apart from formalised religion, mankind is naturally inclined to worship. To worship God is a law of the universe, for He is our Creator, and we are His creation. However, while we have been created with a propensity to worship, directing our worship to God is not compulsory. We were created to be free moral agents, therefore, we can direct our worship elsewhere, if we so choose. If we do not worship God, inevitably, we will set up our own idols, and these can take many forms. For example, money, fame, power, fashion, materialism, sex, food, body image, mobile phones, video games, social media (the list is endless). The definition of an idol is anything that diverts our worship away from God, our Creator and Sustainer. If there is something in our lives receiving all our attention, available time, effort and concentration, that is our idol. Moreover, the first and second commandments make it clear that anything or anyone (apart from God) that receives our spiritual allegiance, is a false god. Worshiping false gods is a direct contravention of the will of the true God.

Daniel 3:13-15 – The king is furious. He summons Shadrach, Meshach and Abednego. Clearly, Nebuchadnezzar was a rash individual, controlled by his passions; any hint of non-compliance with his commands sends him into a fit of rage. However, he tries to compose himself, and asks the three boys whether it is true they are refusing to worship the Babylonian gods, and bow before the statue. Before they can answer, he tells them he will give them one more chance. The orchestra will strike up again, and if they do not bow, they will be thrown into the blazing furnace. He defiantly demands *"Then what god will be able to rescue you from my hand?"*

Daniel 3:16-18 – The response of the three boys is extraordinary. They show neither fear, nor concern for their lives. They tell the king they have no intention of defending themselves in the matter. If they are thrown into the furnace, the God they serve is able to deliver them from it, for He is powerful enough to save them from any punishment the king cares to order. But, even if God doesn't deliver them, they are informing the king that they will not worship his gods, nor will they worship the golden image.

What an answer! It goes beyond bravery. It shows incredible faith. Surely, this is the faith that moves mountains. The famous *"even if He doesn't"* response is a declaration all Christians aspire to. It proclaims that a Christian will be obedient to God:

- whether He saves them from a difficult situation, or not;
- whether He saves their lives, or not;
- whether He grants them prosperity, or not;
- whether He answers their prayers in the way they want Him to, or not;
- whether they gain favour in the eyes of others, or not;
- whatever the circumstance, they will follow the instructions of their God.

No-where in the account do we see Shadrach, Meshach and Abednego praying for guidance on the matter. This was not an issue necessitating further direction from God. They knew the Ten Commandments, and simply followed them.

Daniel 3:19-23 – At this point, the king completely loses composure, and is beside himself with rage. His face changes; no more Mr Nice King. He is not giving any more chances. He orders that the furnace be heated seven times hotter (as if this will be more menacing than an already blazing furnace). Shadrach, Meshach and Abednego are tied hand and foot, and the result of the furnace's increased temperature is the immediate death of the strong soldiers restraining the boys in front of the fire.

Shadrach, Meshach and Abednego are hurled into the furnace.

Daniel 3:24-25 – Nebuchadnezzar then retires to a viewing area in order to watch the boys burn. However, what he sees makes him jump to his feet. Astonished, he asks *"Weren't there three men that we tied up and threw into the fire?"* His officials confirm that indeed three men were thrown in. Then the king says *"Look! I see four men walking around in the fire, unbound and unharmed, and the fourth looks like a son of the gods."*

The Hebrew boys were prepared to die for their faith. If God allowed them to die in the furnace, they were content, but instead of suffering a terribly painful death God saved their lives and, in addition, sent Jesus to join them in the fire.

There is a saying that God answers every prayer, but His answer may be 'yes', 'no' or 'wait'. We may pray for deliverance, but we must do so believing that God will answer in accordance with His plan for our lives. Therefore, we must trust that whatever His answer, it is for our ultimate benefit. Moreover, He will accompany us through the entire experience. This was certainly a test of faith for Shadrach, Meshach and Abednego that would further strengthen their trust in God. However, the lessons, taught by this amazing event, go far beyond the Hebrew boys. Firstly, it serves as an outstanding testimony of the power of God, and His care for His people, to all who witnessed the event, or who hear, or read the story throughout succeeding generations. Secondly, it reminds us that God will often take our experience to the wire in order to maximise the impact of the rescue. Thirdly, Nebuchadnezzar was able to see Jesus, which had a massive effect on him. He had heard of Daniel's God, but now he was privileged to see Him for himself. God is targeting Nebuchadnezzar's heart.

Daniel 3:26-27 – The king approaches the furnace and shouts to Shadrach, Meshach and Abednego, calling them *"servants of the Most High God",* and ordering them to come out. The boys obey, and walk out of the fire. They are thoroughly examined by not only the king, but also his satraps, prefects, governors and royal advisors, and are found to be totally unharmed; not a hair is singed; their robes are intact; not even the smell of burning is on them. All the fire has been able to do is burn away the ropes with which they were bound.

Daniel 3:28-30 – The king then praises the God of heaven, as follows:

> *"Praise be to the God of*
> *Shadrach, Meshach and Abednego,*
> *who has sent His angel and rescued his servants!*
> *They trusted in Him and defied the king's command*
> *and were willing to give up their lives*
> *rather than serve or worship any god except their own God."*

Furthermore, the king decrees that any of his subjects, who speak against the God of the Hebrew boys, will be cut into pieces and their houses turned into piles of rubble. For he says *"..no other god can save in this way."*

Then, Nebuchadnezzar gives Shadrach, Meshach and Abednego another promotion.

We have seen this type of response from the king before, and perhaps we are learning to take these proclamations and decrees with a pinch of salt, for they do not appear to signify a lasting conversion. God will have to deal even more dramatically with Nebuchadnezzar, in order to win his heart.

God may choose to deal with us in the same way He dealt with the Hebrew boys. In our everyday lives, even though we pray earnestly, He may not save us from a negative, or even harmful, situation. He may decide to reveal Himself from within the situation. He not only tests our faith, but involves Himself in our challenges. He wants us to learn to trust Him, and in addition, He orchestrates our experience to be a witness to others, so that they might be brought to view Him. We should never underestimate the effect of our experiences on others: the impact is powerful and encouraging, even to those who may have been the cause of the situation. Sometimes, God allows us to lose out to others, in order for them to see Jesus. This is not always an easy encounter, but our faith will certainly become stronger because of it. Therefore, if you are presently praying for deliverance, perhaps from ill health, financial difficulties, people who appear to wish your downfall, and the situation is not being alleviated, think about the declaration of the three Hebrew boys. They knew God was able to deliver them, but were determined to stay faithful to Him, whether He rescued them, or not. They were prepared to die rather than disobey God. The positive effect this type of attitude has on others is immeasurable.

Daniel Chapter Four

THE BIBLICAL WEREWOLF

Based on Daniel 4:1-37

Daniel chapter four is a very unusual letter written by king Nebuchadnezzar.

Daniel 4:1 – The king introduces himself. His letter is to go to *"..the nations and peoples of every language, who live on the earth."* This must be an important letter for it is addressed to the world. He starts with an encouraging greeting *"May you prosper greatly."*

Daniel 4:2-3 – The king wastes no time. He tells the recipients what his letter is about. He writes: *"It is my pleasure to tell you about the miraculous signs and wonders that the Most High God has performed for me.*
> *"How great are His signs,*
> *how mighty His wonders!*
> *His kingdom is an eternal kingdom;*
> *His dominion endures from generation to generation."*

We are used to the king making declarations about the true God. He has done so on three separate occasions (see Daniel 1:19,20, Daniel 2:47, Daniel 3:28,29), but this proclamation is different. This time, the king is speaking of his own experience. Something has happened to Nebuchadnezzar. He is now a worshiper of Daniel's God, and his letter is the testimony of his conversion.

Here is king Nebuchadnezzar's conversion story:

Daniel 4:4-5 - He is at home in his palace, content and prosperous. He isn't troubled; his kingdom is thriving. And, at this peaceful time in his life, God chooses to disturb him with a strange dream that terrifies him.

Daniel 4:6-9 - The dream is so disturbing he summons all his wise men (magicians, enchanters, astrologers and diviners) to interpret it. The king sends for Daniel last of all. We already know, from Daniel chapter two, the king is aware that only Daniel is able to interpret his dreams. Therefore, it is curious that he calls the soothsayers first to see what they will say. Perhaps, the king felt some foreboding about his dream. This time, he did not ask the soothsayers to tell him the dream; he revealed it straightaway. It appears, that in his eagerness to receive a favourable interpretation, he is willing to reveal all. Nebuchadnezzar knows Daniel will tell him the truth, and perhaps he is fearful of this.

Despite being given the dream, the soothsayers have no idea what it means. Therefore, Nebuchadnezzar is forced to call for Daniel.

Daniel 4:10-17 - The king's dream: He saw an enormous tree standing in the middle of the land. It grew large and strong, reaching to the sky, and was visible at the ends of the earth. Its foliage was beautiful. It bore abundant fruit and provided food for, and shelter to, every creature, even the birds lived in its branches. Then he saw an angel fly down from heaven, calling in a loud voice *"Cut down the tree and trim off its branches: strip off its leaves and scatter its fruit. Let the animals flee from under it and the birds from its branches. But let the stump and its roots, bound with iron and bronze, remain in the ground, in the grass of the field. Let him be drenched with the dew of heaven, and let him live with the animals among the plants of the earth. Let his mind be changed from that of a man and let him be given the mind of an animal, till seven times pass by for him."*

The angel then declares why all this must take place. It is so human beings may understand that God is sovereign over all earthly kingdoms. He is the one who sets up the rulers of earth's kingdoms, from the humblest to the greatest. This is the end of the dream.

Daniel 4:18 – Nebuchadnezzar then begs Daniel to reveal the meaning of his dream.

Daniel 4:19-27 – Daniel knows what the dream means, but is reluctant to tell the king. In fact, Daniel is greatly perplexed; he has grown fond of Nebuchadnezzar and does not want the dream to be fulfilled. The king sees the expression on Daniel's face. He prepares himself for bad news, and instructs Daniel to, just say it as it is. Daniel's response shows the depth of their friendship *"My lord, if only the dream applied to your enemies and its meaning to your adversaries!"* Daniel's attitude towards the king is a powerful message to us. Daniel had been forced into captivity, castrated, and made to officiate in the court of the king of his captors. Yet, he has developed a fond relationship with his enemy, to the point where he is now unhappy at the prospect of Nebuchadnezzar's predicted misfortune.

We may find ourselves trapped in unfavourable situations, unpleasant work environments we cannot escape, rubbing shoulders daily with people who treat us harshly, but a Christian must try to find a way to love the unlovable, give them our very best service, and sincerely wish them well (See 1 Peter 2:18).

Daniel gives the interpretation:
As the king already suspects, the great tree that touched the sky and provided food and shelter for every creature, represents Nebuchadnezzar himself. He has indeed become great and strong, and his greatness has grown until it reaches the sky, with his dominion extending to distant parts of the earth. The directive from the angel will be carried out against the king. He will be driven away from people to live as a wild animal among the beasts. He will eat grass like an ox, and live outdoors drenched by the dew. After seven years he will regain his sanity, and acknowledge that God is sovereign over all kingdoms on earth, and He gives them to anyone He wishes. The angel's command that the

stump and root of the tree must remain, indicates the king will be restored to his throne, and will then worship the true God.

Daniel knows God is merciful, so advises the king to repent of his sins immediately, rule fairly, and show kindness to the oppressed. Daniel is certain this change in the king's attitude, and behaviour, will make the fulfilment of the dream unnecessary. He believes, if the king repents, God will change His mind.

It may seem strange to acknowledge that an infallible God can change His mind, but in many instances in the Bible, we see God giving warnings of calamity and catastrophe, then relenting when the people repent and turn from doing evil. (See Ezekiel 33:11, Jonah 3). Surely, this contradicts the perception of an arbitrary or tyrannical God. As Psalm 103:8,10,11 confirm, *"The Lord is compassionate and gracious, slow to anger, abounding in love. He does not treat us as our sins deserve or repay us according to our iniquities. For as high as the heavens are above the earth, so great is His love for those who fear Him."*

Daniel 4:28-30 - No doubt, king Nebuchadnezzar made every effort to live by goodly principles following Daniel's appeal, but unfortunately his improved behaviour did not last. Twelve months later, he is walking on the roof of the palace, looking out over the magnificent palatial structures and beautiful gardens, and declares *"Is not this the great Babylon I have built as the royal residence, by my mighty power and for the glory of my majesty?"* What a statement! Too soon, the king had forgotten the true God of heaven, and that only through His power and grace can we achieve anything on this earth. The king was ascribing 'glory' and 'majesty' to himself rather than to Almighty God. Full of vanity and pride, the king had committed blasphemy.

Daniel 4:31-32 – Whilst he is still speaking, Nebuchadnezzar hears a voice from heaven saying:

"This is what is decreed for you, king Nebuchadnezzar. Your royal authority has been taken from you. You will be driven away from people and will live with the wild animals; you will eat grass like the ox. Seven times will pass by for you until you acknowledge that the Most High is sovereign over all kingdoms on earth and gives them to anyone He wishes."

Daniel 4:33 - And immediately, what was predicted came true. For seven years a madness came over the king that caused him to look, and live, like an animal - a Biblical werewolf. He walked on all fours, his hair became matted like eagle feathers, and his nails grew into bird claws. He had to be driven from his palace, and lived in the fields eating grass, and running with the wild animals. No doubt, the whole scene was viewed by his court officials, servants, and subjects, who had previously bowed to him, paid him homage, and carried out his commands. What a curiosity, and how humiliating.

Daniel 4:34-36 - The story has a happy ending. After seven years of trotting like an animal, with his head bowed to the ground, king Nebuchadnezzar looked up towards heaven, and the madness left him. He praised, honoured and glorified the most high, eternal God, with the words:

> *"His dominion is an eternal dominion;*
> *His kingdom endures from generation to generation.*
> *All peoples of the earth*
> *are regarded as nothing.*
> *He does as He pleases*
> *with the powers of heaven*
> *and the peoples of the earth.*
> *No one can hold back His hand*
> *or say to Him. "What have You done?"*

The king not only regained his sanity but also all the honour, splendour and glory of his kingdom; for his advisers and nobles sought him out, he was restored to his throne, and commanded even greater respect than before.

Daniel 4:37 – Nebuchadnezzar concludes his letter with a fitting epilogue. He now praises, exalts, and glorifies, the King of heaven (not himself). He admits that everything God does is right, and all His ways are just. He is able to humble all those who walk in pride.

An astounding story.

It is unfortunate that some of us have to be brought down a peg or two before we acknowledge that God is the God of gods, King of kings, and Lord of lords. The power of God is something to be marvelled at. Whilst we have been given the freedom to choose to do good or evil, God has the power to set up kings and depose them. He is able to convert men into animals, and restore them to sane human beings. As William Cowper's hymn says: *"God moves in a mysterious way, His wonders to perform."* He does all this in an effort to save our souls. If we are obstinate and fight against Him, God may need to resort to more extreme measures to get our attention. But once we give in, and accept Him as King of our lives, He is then able to lavish blessings on us, and restore us to the high places of the world and, in the end, grant us eternal life.

No longer is Nebuchadnezzar talking about the God of Daniel and the Hebrew boys. He is talking about his God. He has been converted in the most dramatic of ways. The last we see of Nebuchadnezzar in the book of Daniel, is his attempt to evangelise the world with the story of how God turned him into a Biblical werewolf, and humbled him in order to exalt him, and save him.

Daniel Chapter Five

WEIGHED IN THE BALANCES

Based on Daniel 5:1-31

In Daniel chapter five we are introduced to king Belshazzar, the grandson of Nebuchadnezzar. Following Nebuchadnezzar's death, his son, Nabonidus, and grandson, Belshazzar, ruled Babylon jointly. It is now 539BC and the kingdom of Babylon is being threatened by the allied nations of Medes and Persians.

Daniel 5:1 – It is at this precarious time in Babylon's history that king Belshazzar decides to hold a great banquet for a thousand of his nobles. Under the prevailing circumstances this was certainly an unusual move.

Cyrus, the king of Persia, had marched against Babylon, and king Nabonidus met him with his forces at the city of Opis, situated on the river Tigris. Nabonidus fought with Cyrus in an effort to prevent the Persians crossing the river. But Cyrus defeated the Babylonian king, and pressed through to Sippar on the river Euphrates. Cyrus captured Sippar without a fight in October 539BC. Nabonidus then fled south, but his son Belshazzar stayed in Babylon (35 miles south of Sippar) believing its strong fortifications would be enough to save the Babylonians from the Persians. ('Bible Study Guide – Daniel' 2004, page 54)

Surrounded, as he was, by the Persian army, why would Belshazzar hold a banquet? Perhaps it was a show of strength, or a desperate act of defiance, perhaps an attempt to raise the confidence of his nobles, or even a final revelry before defeat.

Daniel 5:2-4 – The young and inexperienced king is certainly worried. At the banquet, the wine is flowing, and he is getting drunk in an effort to drown his sorrows. In his drunken state he decides to do something very rash. He calls for the gold and silver goblets, confiscated by his grandfather from the temple in Jerusalem. These goblets were holy; dedicated to the worship of Jehovah, they had been set aside for religious use only. Belshazzar, his nobles, wives and concubines proceed to drink fermented wine from the sacred vessels. Intoxicated as they are, they use the vessels to offer toasts to the gold, silver, bronze, iron, wood and stone Babylonian idol gods.

In his desperation, Belshazzar toasts every god he can think of. If the consecrated goblets held some secret power, perhaps they would help to ward off the Persian army. The king and his guests were certainly seeking something from the gods. They must have reasoned that the combination of the sacred goblets, and their drunken toasts to the gods of gold, silver, bronze, iron, wood and stone, could do no harm, and might even improve their situation.

Daniel 5:5-6 - The God of the Jews is the only deity to answer their drunken petition.

Suddenly, giant supernatural fingers of a man's hand appear, and write an inscription on the wall of the banquet hall. Belshazzar sobers up at once. He turns pale, his knees knock together, and his legs give way. The king is terrified. He realises he has desecrated the holy goblets. Belshazzar knows his grandfather's conversion story, yet here he is, defying the God who turned Nebuchadnezzar into an animal for seven years. The appearance of a dismembered hand writing on his palace wall had to be a terrible warning meant just for him.

Daniel 5:7-8 – Like his grandfather before him, Belshazzar summons the wise men (enchanters, astrologers and diviners). They are promised fine clothes, a gold chain of office, and promotion to the third highest position in the kingdom. These intellectuals, paid to translate these types of messages, are brought in, but once again, they are baffled. They can neither read the inscription, nor give its meaning.

Daniel 5:9 - Belshazzar becomes even more frightened, and again the blood drains from his face. No-one, including his nobles, know what to do. He feels a foreboding that the message on the wall spells his doom, but how can he form a plan of escape if he does not know what it says?

Daniel 5:10-12 - It took a woman to bring some common sense to the situation. The Bible describes her as the queen, but she was obviously not one of Belshazzar's wives or concubines; they were all in the banquet with him. So, this very wise woman, who remembered Daniel, and what he had done for Nebuchadnezzar, could have been his mother, or even his grandmother (Nebuchadnezzar's wife). She hears all the commotion coming from the banquet hall and enters to see what is happening. She sees the agitation of the king, respectfully calms him down, and reminds him there is a man, in his kingdom, filled with the spirit of the holy gods. Of course, she is referring to Daniel. She calls Daniel by his Hebrew name, and recounts to Belshazzar the occasions when Daniel interpreted dreams, explained riddles and solved difficult problems for his grandfather. Daniel is around 83 years old at this time, and in retirement, but his exemplary reputation is remembered. The queen confidently assures the king, Daniel will be able to interpret the writing on the wall.

Those not familiar with this Bible story may not realise it is the origin of the phrase *'the writing is on the wall'*, meaning, here is a sign of something catastrophic about to happen.

Daniel 5:13-16 – Daniel is summoned, and the king brings him up to speed with everything that has happened, adding, that if he is able to give the meaning of the supernatural message, he will be rewarded with fine clothes, a gold chain of office, and promotion to the third highest position in the kingdom.

Daniel 5:17 – Daniel has heard it all before. He tells the king to keep all the promised rewards; he does not need them. However, he will interpret the message.

Daniel 5:18-21 – As usual, Daniel must give glory to God before carrying out a task for the king. He recounts to Belshazzar the entire repentance story of his grandfather. He reminds Belshazzar that Nebuchadnezzar was the undisputed ruler of the world with matchless power, splendour and wealth. He tells of how Nebuchadnezzar foolishly took credit for all God had blessed him with, until God humbled him by turning him into an animal.

Daniel 5:22-24 – Now, Daniel contrasts the experience of Nebuchadnezzar with that of Belshazzar. He tells the king that although he was clearly aware of his grandfather's story, it has had no effect. He has not learned humility. Instead, he has set himself up against the Lord of heaven. His act of bringing out the sacred goblets for his nobles, wives and concubines to drink fermented wine, and give praise to false gods, is the last straw. Belshazzar has not honoured the God who holds his life in His hands. Therefore, the God he has rejected has sent this message for him.

We cannot order our lives solely by our own experiences. If we are wise, we will carefully consider the lives of others as well. When we hear their testimonies, read their stories, or witness their actions, we can determine what is prudent and beneficial for us. Because their experiences have not happened to us personally, we should not ignore them. Many people have gained salvation through the stories of others. As we read the Bible narratives, or hear the accounts of our peers regarding how God has dealt with them, we will become curious about how He can benefit our lives. Belshazzar's knowledge of his grandfather's experience, together with the events of his own life, were enough for him to make a decision to follow the God of heaven. Despite his knowledge of all that had gone before, he chose not to repent of his evil way of life. God had given him ample time to reform, and now he was without excuse.

Daniel 5:25-28 - Here is the supernatural inscription:

M N M N T Q L P R S N

It is written in Hebrew consonants only. That is why the Babylonian soothsayers could not decipher it.

Daniel has no problem reading the message; he had received his deciphering skills from the Person who wrote it. Daniel inserts the correct vowels and separates the words, as follows:

MENE   MENE   TEKEL   PARSIN

These are the names of common weights used on weighing scales. So translated in modern terms, they read:

A pound. A pound. An ounce. Half an ounce.

God's message to Belshazzar is a play on words. Written in weight names, it cleverly hints that something (or someone) is being weighed on spiritual scales.

Daniel interprets the weight names as:

Numbered. Numbered. Weighed. Divided.

Then gives the full message represented by the weights:

- Your days are **numbered** and brought to an end (this is repeated for emphasis);
- Your days are **numbered** and brought to an end;
- You have been **weighed** in the balances and found wanting;
- Your kingdom is **divided** and given to the Medes and Persians.

The consonants for the word **Parsin, PRSN**, can also be translated as **PERES** or **PARAS,** the Hebrew word for Persian. God is giving another hint: the Persian kingdom will be involved in the dividing of Babylon. ('Bible Study Guide – Daniel' 2004, page 60)

Unfortunately for Belshazzar, his time for repentance had passed. The prophecy was fulfilled that very night.

That night, king Cyrus created a dam diverting the river Euphrates. This caused the water level to drop as it flowed beneath the Babylonian city wall. When the river level reached thigh height, the Persian army was able to enter the city along the river bed under the city wall. Furthermore, as prophesied around 150 years earlier in Isaiah 45:1, the inner gates of the city were left unlocked on that fateful night. That night, Belshazzar was killed, but his father Nabonidus, who had previously fled south, was spared by Cyrus, and granted residence in a Persian province. (Herodotus, 'The Histories') Babylon was overthrown by the Persian army just as revealed by Daniel.

Daniel 5:27 (NKJV) states *"You have been weighed in the balances, and found wanting."* It was God's pronouncement on Belshazzar, but it could just as easily be pronounced on any one of us today. God is saying, 'Your life does not measure up to My standard. You are not up to scratch.' None of us knows when our time is up; when our days will be numbered and brought to an end.

We can only live each day as if it might be our last, because the truth is, that could be the case.

Later, in our study of Daniel, we will read about the Investigative Judgement, which is the judgement of God's people taking place in heaven right now. In fact, as we speak, someone's book is under heavenly scrutiny. Whenever our individual cases are judged, we will not be aware of it; as we will not be present to witness it. Every one of us has a book of our deeds, which is faithfully completed by our recording angel each day. This is the book that will speak for us in the judgement (see Revelation 20:12). Our cases will be decided in our absence, and without our knowledge. That is why we have no time to lose. Jesus came to this earth and died so that we can all gain eternal life. Entering into a love relationship with Him is the only way we can be pronounced 'not guilty' in the heavenly court session presently taking place.

Belshazzar's tragic story brings to our attention the issues we should all be considering 'Could the writing be on the wall for me today?' 'Could I be weighed in the balances and found wanting?' 'Is the time for my repentance at an end?' The Bible tells us, a time of reckoning is appointed for everyone. Just like Belshazzar, we must all face the consequences of our actions (see Ecclesiastes 12:13,14). How wonderful that Jesus has already paid the price for our sins, and that if we ask Him, God will forgive us for our misdeeds, cover us with Jesus' righteous character, and pardon us.

Daniel 5:29-31 – The chapter ends informing us that Belshazzar did indeed reward Daniel with the royal robe, gold chain and promotion; which, of course, proved academic, as that very night Belshazzar was killed and Darius, the 62 year old king of the Medes, took over the Babylonian kingdom.

Daniel Chapter Six

WE HAVE TO BE CHRISTIANS AT WORK TOO

Based on Daniel 6:1-28

As we saw in Daniel chapter five, Babylon was overthrown by Cyrus, the Persian king, in 539BC. Cyrus had made an alliance with Darius, king of the Medes, and it was Darius who took up rulership of the defeated Babylonian kingdom.

Daniel 6:1-2 - Usually, an incoming king would put to death, not only the defeated king, but also his noblemen and officials. However, in this case, Darius decides to put in place 120 satraps (governors of provinces) to rule over individual areas. These satraps were answerable to three administrators, one of whom was Daniel. Therefore, Daniel was a senior manager over 40 middle managers, and answered only to the king.

Daniel 6:3 - Daniel is a Jew, he is 83 years old and retired, yet the Mede king appoints him as a senior statesman. This decision was certainly controversial. Yet Darius has good judgement, for Daniel turns out to be the best of the three administrators. He distinguishes himself among both the administrators and the satraps. The king recognises Daniel has exceptional qualities, and plans to further promote him to be ruler over the whole kingdom.

Daniel 6:4 – The other administrators and satraps see what is happening and decide to put a stop to it by finding grounds for charges against Daniel in his conduct of government affairs. However, they fail to find anything against him. All they discover is that he is trustworthy, and above reproach. He cannot be bribed, neither is he negligent in any of his duties. He carries out his work to perfection.

How do you perform in the workplace? What do your workmates think of you? Could they find grounds on which to accuse you regarding the way you work, and the service you give? The Bible advises that everything we do should bring glory to God (see I Corinthians 10:31, Colossians 3:23, Ephesians 6:7). In other words, we must carry out each duty, and each task, as if we are doing it for God; to the best of our ability, and to the highest standard possible. There are times when we feel ill treated by our employer, and are caught up in feelings of hatred and anger towards work colleagues, because of the way they interact with us, or even through a clash of personalities. But, should we then return evil for evil; or give poor service? Will this response improve our situation? Daniel had every right to give less than his best in his job. He didn't want to be there. He desperately wished to be back in Jerusalem. He had been brought to Babylon against his will. Yet, he had served Nebuchadnezzar to such a degree that the king had become his friend. Daniel came to like, and respect king Nebuchadnezzar, and wish him only good fortune. Then, Babylon was overthrown, and instead of Daniel being allowed to return to Jerusalem, he was made to serve the new conquerors. It was like being taken into captivity all over again. Yet, Daniel did not complain or lament his misfortune; he decided to once again give his very best service. Was Daniel consorting with the enemy? No, he was being a true Christian.

Despite any mistreatment received from your employer, you can still serve them faithfully. The way to deal with a bad employer is not to rebel against them, behave with truculence, tell them off, or 'bad-mouth' them to your colleagues, friends and family. Daniel is our example. Give good service, and look for opportunities to be a blessing in the workplace. Remember, the way of the world is to retaliate. Therefore, if you truly wish to make a positive impact in your place of work, you should act differently to the norm; give your unfair manager behaviour they are not expecting; return exemplary service for bad treatment.

For Christians, the required standard of behaviour is even higher. The Christian's mission is to spread the gospel in order to give others the opportunity to get to know Jesus, and be saved. They are to love their neighbours as themselves. If they are disrespecting their employers, and rebelling against perceived unfair treatment, they cannot carry out these basic Christian principles.

If you have an unfair boss, one course of action might be to try to find out why your boss (or employer) is mistreating you. You could ask yourself 'Am I doing something to contribute to this situation? Is there something I can do to alleviate the problem?' Taking responsibility for your part, and seeking what you can do, is a positive way of handling the issue. Remember, we are instructed by the Bible that whatever the situation, we must give our very best service. This is a challenge, but no-one said the Christian way of life is easy. It certainly isn't. God promises He will not leave us on our own; He knows we do not possess the ability to repay evil with good. Therefore, He sends the Holy Spirit to give us the power, and grace, to live a life worthy of the name Christian (see Romans 8:14).

Daniel 6:5 - After observing Daniel, the satraps and administrators decide the only way they can bring about his downfall is through his adherence to the law of God. How did they know this? Daniel must have made his worship of God very open and plain to everyone. He did not keep it a secret. Everyone knew Daniel would never act against God's law. They witnessed his worship habits. They saw Daniel did not compromise when it came to his faith.

For Christians, it may not be easy to let everyone know we are people of faith, but we certainly should not be trying to hide the fact. Remember, the Christian's mission is to spread the gospel. This does not necessarily mean we should be preaching to our workmates, but our behaviour within the workplace should reflect our Christian principles. Moreover, as we chat with our colleagues, we will naturally find opportunities to share details of our faith and practice. If our workmates have no idea we are Christians, something is wrong.

Daniel's workmates realised he was blameless. The Bible definition of someone who lives a blameless life, is not, a perfect individual, but rather someone who enjoys a vibrant, close and loving relationship with God.

Here are some of Daniel's qualities:
- Daniel 1:8 – He obeyed the health laws;
- Daniel 2:23 – He had God-given wisdom and power;
- Daniel 2:26-28 – He always gave credit to God;
- Daniel 2:49 – He looked out for his friends;
- Daniel 4:19 – He made friends of his enemies;
- Daniel 5:11 - He had the spirit of God in him and was known for this;
- Daniel 5:17 – He was not interested in worldly honour or riches.

It is possible for us to be like Daniel. Our relationship with God, that leads us to want to be like Him in every way, is what designates us as blameless.

What do your workmates see when they observe you? Do they know that the only charge they can level against you is to do with your faithful worship of God? Or are they able to point out lots of petty misdemeanours in your performance?

Daniel 6:6-8 - As seen in this story, even when we are doing our very best in the workplace, and worshiping God in every way we can, there are still people who will seek to harm us. The administrators and satraps, knowing they could only attack Daniel through his faithfulness to God, hatched a dastardly plan. They formed a delegation, and appealed to the king's vanity.

Having a group of work colleagues conspire against you is not a pleasant experience. Daniel chapter six continually refers to Daniel's workmates acting against him *"as a group"*. People may well choose to form alliances in order to do evil. They feel emboldened when acting in unison with others. A group will often do things an individual would not feel brave enough to carry out. It is good to remember that the majority is frequently wrong. We need to act in accordance with our own conscience. If we are afraid to carry out a dubious action on our own, forming a group to carry out the action, may not be the right way forward.

The delegation of administrators and satraps pretended to have the backing of all the king's officials. They proposed that Darius issue a decree that, for the next 30 days, all the prayers of his subjects be directed only to him. Anyone found disobeying this law should be thrown into the lions' den.

The law the administrators and satraps were requesting was completely without rhyme or reason. There was no need for it at all, except that it stroked the king's ego; only he would be worshiped for the next 30 days. In other words, for one month he would be honoured above all gods (including Daniel's God).

Daniel 6:9 – King Darius, blinded by his own pride and vanity, does not take the time to think things through. Straightaway he has the decree drawn up. And, according to the law of the Medes and Persians, any written law could not be altered or repealed. Of course, the administrators and satraps know this, and are counting on it.

Daniel 6:10 – The king's decree totally opposed the law of God. The Ten Commandments state that God, the Creator, is the only one to be worshiped (see Exodus 20:3,8).

Daniel learns of the king's decree and immediately realises the implications, but in his eyes he has no choice. From the age of 17, he made a pact with his friends to obey God despite the consequences. He has lived his life in this way, and now is not the time to relent. He knows if he obeys the law of the king he will break the Ten Commandments. And, although he could have prayed in secret, so as not to offend the king, Daniel chose to stay faithful to God and continue his practice of praying three times a day with his windows open towards Jerusalem.

It is interesting that Daniel was so public in his praying habits, especially in the light of Jesus' instruction that we should pray in secret (see Matthew 6:6). However, when we read the context of Jesus' teachings we see He is talking about making public prayers in order to show others how holy we are (see Matthew 6:1-8). This was not what Daniel was doing. He had a close personal relationship with God, therefore he communicated with Him three times a day. Moreover, he faced Jerusalem when he prayed because, many years before the Babylonian captivity, king Solomon had prayed *"...Hear the supplication of Your servant and of Your people Israel when they pray toward this place."* (1 Kings 8:30). Daniel was following the practice of the Jews to pray towards Jerusalem where the temple of God had been situated. For Daniel to halt this practice would have been to compromise his allegiance to God. If he had always prayed in secret then he could have continued doing so. However, to change his practice now, would have been to obey the king rather than God, thus signalling a victory for the satraps and administrators. He had to be true to his God despite the threat of death. Daniel well understood the intention of his jealous colleagues, but he chose to make a public stand for God, just as Shadrach, Meshach and Abednego had done, so many years before.

God asks His people to be consistent, whether in times of peace and prosperity, or times of hardship. We must continually trust in Him. Our Christian practice must not be dependent on circumstance, or consequence.

Daniel 6:11 – The administrators and satraps set up a group stake out. They do not have to wait long. As usual, Daniel opens his windows towards Jerusalem, and they witness him praying to God; petitioning Him for help.

Daniel 6:12-14 – The group of administrators and satraps hurry back to report to the king. First, they ask him *"Did you not publish a decree that during the next 30 days anyone who prays to any god or human being except to you, Your Majesty, would be thrown into the lions' den?"* The king, who still has not realised the trap set for him, answers *"The decree stands in accordance with the law of the Medes and Persians, and cannot be repealed."* Now it is time to spring the trap. They tell the king *"Daniel, who is one of the exiles from Judah, pays no attention to you, Your Majesty, or to the decree you put in writing. He still prays three times a day."*

Too late, king Darius realises the cost of his vanity. He is once again reminded by the group of accusers that the law of the Medes and Persians cannot be repealed. And, although, as king, he could have chosen to repeal his own law, he doesn't. He was the king, he could do anything he wished, but his reputation was at stake. To repeal the law would be to admit he had been outwitted by his statesmen; that he had acted in folly, and been tricked. This he felt he could not do.

Our pride can prevent us from stepping down, and admitting we have erred. However, acknowledging a mistake takes greater courage than sticking with a bad decision. Brownie points are not awarded for pretending to be right when you know you are wrong. In fact, by not admitting his error, the king appeared weak in the eyes of the statesmen. They now knew he could be manipulated. If he had stood up to them and repealed the law, they would have lost the power to control him. It is the same with us. People who know us well may press our buttons knowing which way we will jump. We can choose not to give them that power. If we realise we have not acted as we should, instead of trying to defend the misdemeanour, the better course, is to admit we have

51

done wrong, and stand for what is right. Character is strengthened by such action.

The king likes Daniel, and is greatly distressed by the situation. Throughout the day, he attempts to find some loophole that will save Daniel from the penalty for breaking his decree, which is death in the lions' den. But, he fails. It is interesting that Daniel has made a friend of king Darius as well. It appears, wherever he finds himself, Daniel makes friends and influences people, even his enemies.

Daniel 6:15 – At sundown, right on cue, the administrators and satraps come, as a group, to the king and remind him no law of the Medes and Persians can be repealed.

Daniel 6:16-17 - So reluctantly, Darius has Daniel brought to him and, with these words, gives the order for him to be thrown into the lions' den *"May your God, whom you serve continually, rescue you!"* A great stone, sealed with the signet ring of the king, and the rings of his nobles, is placed over the mouth of the den. There is no way anyone can rescue Daniel during the night, not even the king himself. Darius is forced to look to God for a solution. He recognises it is all in God's hands now, and he hopes, and no doubt prays, that Daniel's God will do something miraculous.

Daniel 6:18 - Darius has a miserable evening. He cannot eat, and sends away the entertainment he usually enjoys. He suffers a sleepless night, worrying about Daniel's fate.

Daniel 6:19-22 – At the first light of dawn, Darius rushes to the lions' den. In an anguished voice he calls out *"Daniel, servant of the living God, has your God, whom you serve continually, been able to rescue you from the lions?"* Immediately Daniel answers *"May the king live forever! My God sent His angel,* *and he shut the mouths of the lions. They have not hurt me, because I was found innocent in His sight. Nor have I ever done any wrong before you, Your Majesty."*

Just as with Shadrach, Meshach and Abednego, God did not prevent the trial. Daniel had to spend the night being circled by hungry lions. He had no idea if God would preserve his life, but once in the den, he must have marvelled at the behaviour of the lions. He could see they wanted to attack him, but for some reason they kept their distance. Daniel concluded that an angel was present in the den, invisible to him, but visible to the lions. The angel set up a perimeter around Daniel, which the lions could not cross. Once again, God delivered his servant in the trial, not from the trial.

It is interesting how God rewards our faith. We pray for deliverance, He grants endurance. As we have already seen, He does this, not only to increase our trust in Him, but because He is also seeking the hearts of those looking on. He uses our experience to save others. God sought the salvation of Nebuchadnezzar through the experience of the three Hebrew boys, and now He is seeking the salvation of Darius through the experience of Daniel. He will do the same with us. If you are experiencing hardship at work, instead of praying to be delivered out of the trial, why not ask God to be with you in the trial, so that someone else may be saved. Remember, your bad experience is never all about you.

Daniel 6:23 – The king is overjoyed. Daniel is lifted out of the den, and found to be completely unharmed, not even his clothes are damaged.

Daniel 6:24 – What about the scheming officials? The king orders that all Daniel's accusers be thrown into the lions' den together with their wives and children. The hungry lions, deprived of their meal throughout the night, are more than ready for their morning feed. Before the administrators and satraps (and their families) reach the floor of the den, they are pounced on, and their bones crushed by the ravenous lions. In Old Testament times, the practice of executing the family of a guilty individual, along with the perpetrator, was widely practised. Family members were viewed as being complicit in the perpetrator's actions. This appears to be an attempt to rid the land of the evil, root and branch.

Daniel 6:25-27 – The king's response to the miracle is to write a letter to *"all nations and peoples of every language in all the earth."* The king of the world sends out a decree to all his subjects:

> *"I issue a decree that in every part of my kingdom*
> *people must fear and reverence the God of Daniel.*
> *For He is the living God*
> *and He endures forever:*
> *His kingdom will not be destroyed,*
> *His dominion will never end.*
> *He rescues and He saves;*
> *He performs signs and wonders*
> *in the heavens and on the earth.*
> *He has rescued Daniel*
> *from the power of the lions."*

Although Darius is acknowledging the supremacy of God, we can see from the edict, he has a little way to go in his understanding of the Creator. The decree commands his subjects to worship God. Of course, this is not God's way; He cannot accept forced worship. God has given us the gift of free will, so we may choose to love and worship Him in response to His love for us (see John 3:16). Worshiping God is a conscious choice that can only be made by free individuals. Darius did not understand this yet, but just as with king Nebuchadnezzar, we hope the lesson was eventually learned, and we will see king Darius in heaven.

Daniel 6:28 – This verse confirms Daniel's restoration to high office. It tells us, his political career continued to prosper, not only during the reign of king Darius, but also under the rule of the next king, Cyrus the Persian.

Those who find themselves targeted by jealous and malicious colleagues, and choose to follow the principles of God anyway, can certainly find encouragement in this extraordinary story. Our adherence to Christian practices may bring us into difficult and even dangerous situations, but we can trust in God's love and care for us. He looks after His children, and rewards their fidelity. He promises He will restore them to the high places of society (see Isaiah 58:14).

Footnote:

There was another time in history when a tomb was secured with a stone and an official seal. Matthew 27:57-61, 65-66 tell us the tomb in which Jesus was laid was covered with a great stone and sealed with a Roman seal. We all know what happened to that stone on Easter morning. An angel hit it with such force that he caused an earthquake, which broke the seal, and rolled the stone away from the entrance. The angel then sat on the stone in triumph (Matthew 28:2). The vain attempts of men (influenced by the devil) to keep God's people in the grave will always fail. The devil could not keep Lazarus in the grave; for Jesus raised him from the dead (see John 11:38-44). The devil could not keep Jesus in the grave (see Matthew 28:1-10), and, at the Second Advent, he will not be able to keep the righteous people of God in their graves (see 1 Thessalonians 4:16-18). The devil may cause us to be persecuted because of our faith, but whether God's people are put into a lions' den, with a stone and a seal, or martyred for their beliefs, as many have been, he does not possess power over death (see Revelation 1:18). Only Jesus has the keys of death and hell. And He will bring His people forth, saving them out of the den (like Daniel), raising them from the dead to continue living (like Lazarus), or resurrecting them on the last day when He returns to earth (the First Resurrection – see Revelation 20:5,6). God is all-powerful and He is able to rescue us, or raise us. He is worthy of our praise!

Daniel Chapter Seven

FOUR BEASTS AND A TALKING HORN

Based on Daniel 7:1-28

In Daniel chapter seven, Daniel has a dream, which is an amplified version of Nebuchadnezzar's dream in Daniel chapter two. From now on, we will find Daniel is given more detailed views of the Daniel chapter two dream. God gave an overview in Daniel 2, and is now homing in on various parts of that dream to highlight important issues. Thus, we learn more about the battle between good and evil throughout earth's history – this battle is often called 'the great controversy' and refers to the age old struggle between God and the devil for the allegiance of human beings. The devil uses both political and religious powers to fight against God's people; and we are introduced to his methods in Daniel chapter seven.

Daniel receives his dream in 553BC; the first year of Belshazzar's joint rule over Babylon with his father Nabonidus (Belshazzar was the king who saw the writing on the wall in Daniel chapter five). Therefore, it was before Daniel was thrown into the lion's den by Darius, king of the Medes (see Daniel 6). Daniel was given the dream around 50 years after king Nebuchadnezzar's dream (see Daniel 2). Both dreams cover the same time period – 605BC to Jesus' second coming. Bible prophecy is one very strong argument for believing the Bible is indeed the word of God, for it is always fulfilled exactly as written, and can be verified by history.

Daniel 2 portrays the political world ruling empires. Daniel 7 introduces the religious power that emerges from one of these empires, which is important in the great controversy.

So, let us look at this dream.   Like Daniel 2, it is a prophecy that has great significance for modern times, and for God's people in particular.

Bible prophecy often includes symbols. In order for us to grasp the message, God paints vivid pictures and images to be interpreted. But we need not worry, for the Bible itself gives us the interpretation.

Daniel 7:1 – In Belshazzar's first year as king of Babylon, Daniel has a dream which he faithfully records.

Daniel 7:2 - The dream begins with *"the four winds of heaven churning up the great sea"*. The four winds originate from the compass points north, south, east and west, indicating the dream's global perspective. The scene gives our first prophetic symbols. Jeremiah 25:31-33 tell us that 'winds' represent turmoil amongst nations. Isaiah 57:20 says 'sea' signifies wicked people in unrest.   Revelation 17:15 tells us 'waters' symbolise peoples, multitudes, nations and languages.

Daniel 7:3 - Then, Daniel sees four great beasts, each different from the other, come up out of the sea. Here is our next prophetic symbol. Daniel 7:17 explains the four beasts represent four earthly kingdoms. So putting this all together, Daniel's dream shows four earthly kingdoms that each come to power through war (turmoil amongst nations). They emerge from densely populated multi-national regions.

These four earthly kingdoms are the same four kingdoms we encountered in Daniel 2. We know this because Daniel 2:44 shows that after the four world ruling empires, the first of which is Babylon, the kingdom of God will be set up. And in Daniel 7:17,18 we are told that after the four kingdoms shown in this chapter, the kingdom of the Most High will be set up. Therefore, in Daniel 7, the four kingdoms that exist before the kingdom of God is set up, must be the same four kingdoms shown in Daniel 2 – Babylon, Medo-Persia, Greece, Rome.

Here are the descriptions of the four beasts Daniel sees in his dream representing the four world ruling nations:

Daniel 7:4 – A lion with wings of an eagle. This is the nation of Babylon (605BC-539BC): the first world ruling empire.

Babylon conducted its conquests with the ferocity of a lion, and with the speed of a flying eagle. Habakkuk 1:6-8 describes Babylon as *"...ruthless and impetuous..... they sweep across the whole earth to seize dwellings not their own. They are a feared and dreaded people; they are a law to themselves..."*

Although the city of Babylon no longer exists today, archaeological remains found in Iraq (the modern site of ancient Babylon) show that one of the most popular symbols used in Babylonian carvings and statues was that of a mighty winged lion. This gives further support to the identity of the first beast Daniel sees in his dream.

Daniel sees the lion's wings torn off. It is then lifted from the ground, stands on two feet like a man, and gains the heart of a man. You will remember in Daniel 4, how king Nebuchadnezzar became an animal, living with beasts, and running around the fields on all fours. Then in Daniel 4:34, as prophesied, he regained his sanity, returned to being a man, stood up on his two legs, walked back into his palace, and once again took his place as ruler of the then known world. No doubt, Daniel 7 is referring to this event when it says, the lion *"stood on two feet like a human being, and the mind of a human was given to it."*

Daniel 7:5 – The second beast Daniel sees is a bear, raised up on one of its sides. It has three ribs between its teeth and is instructed to get up and eat its fill of flesh.

If the lion is Babylon, then **the bear that follows it must be Medo-Persia (539BC-331BC),** which overthrew Babylon and became the second world ruling empire. This kingdom was formed of an alliance between the Medes and Persians; the Persians being the stronger of the two nations. Thus, the bear is shown as raised on one side. The three ribs it holds in its teeth indicate the three great nations overthrown by Medo-Persia, namely, Lydia, Babylon and Egypt. Medo-Persia was a particularly bloodthirsty empire, that in the dream was told to *"get up and eat your fill of flesh."*

Daniel 7:6 – Next, Daniel sees a **leopard with four heads, and four bird's wings on its back. It receives authority to rule. This represents Greece the third world ruling empire that reigned in 331BC-168BC.** The kingdom, led by Alexander the Great, extended as far as India and North East Africa. Alexander would have continued his exploits had his troops not become homesick. He died at the age of 32, probably from fever and exhaustion, caused largely by a life of debauchery. (Wikipedia – Death of Alexander the Great). There is much speculation about the death of Alexander, but it is said he became a drunkard because, after conquering the world, he could find nothing to challenge him. There was nothing left for this brilliant military commander to achieve, and he drank himself to death from boredom.

After Alexander's death, four Greek generals assassinated his relatives and ruled in his stead. The generals are represented by the four heads of the leopard. Revelation 17:9,10 reveal that prophetic beasts with multiple heads indicate multiple rulers. The four generals divided the Greek Empire into four confederacies. As Exodus 19:4 describes the speed with which God led His people as, being borne on wings, similarly, the leopard's four wings indicate the speed with which Alexander conquered the world. Alexander amassed his world empire in just 13 years. (www.ushistory.org/alexanderthegreat)

Daniel 7:7 - Now we come to **the fourth animal Daniel sees in his dream. We are told this beast is very different from the other three. It is terrifying, frightening and very powerful. It has large iron teeth, and ten horns. It crushes and devours its victims and tramples the remainder underfoot.**

As we saw in Daniel 2, this is the fourth world ruling empire, Rome (168BC-AD476). In Nebuchadnezzar's dream (see Daniel 2:33, 40), the legs of the statue are made of iron, which breaks and smashes everything, breaks things to pieces, and crushes and breaks all the others. In Daniel's dream this terrible beast has great iron teeth that *"devour the whole earth, trampling it down and crushing it"* (see Daniel 7:23). History tells us, the Roman Empire was known for its use of iron swords, which were almost invincible against the weapons of other nations. The Roman Empire flourished in the Iron Age. ('Wikipedia – Iron Age')

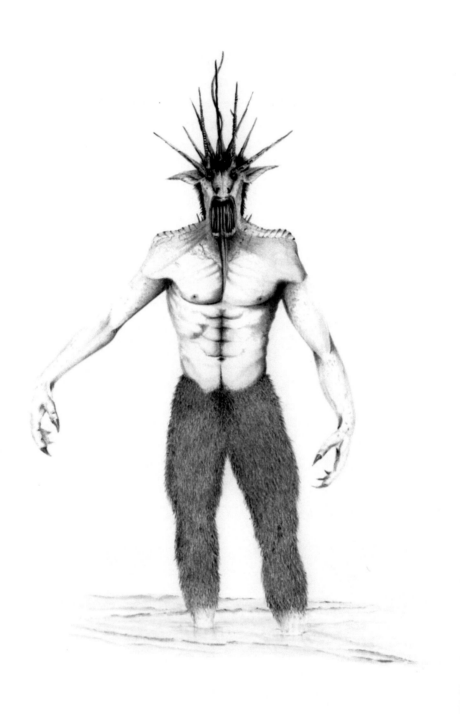

The fourth beast has ten horns. Revelation 17:12 tells us that in Bible prophecy horns on beasts signify kings or rulers. In Daniel 2 the fourth world ruling empire (Rome) was followed by the ten toes, made partly of iron, and partly of clay; some parts weak, some parts strong, ever trying to bond together but never achieving unity. History tells us the Roman Empire was not overthrown by a fifth world ruling empire. It disintegrated. From AD330 Emperor Constantine moved his seat of government from Rome to Constantinople (Istanbul, Turkey), and a long drawn out decline began in the western half of the empire. Roman authority slowly faded away, and was followed by the Barbarian tribes from the north, who attacked the Roman Empire on many different fronts, wearing it down until it broke into smaller kingdoms, some weak and some strong. ('SDA Bible Study Guide - Daniel' 2004 page 80)

The ten horns represent the divided remnants of the Roman Empire ruling in Europe (the same as the ten toes of the Daniel 2 statue). In other words, they represent the nations, largely situated in Europe, that emerged from the Roman Empire. According to history, these ten kingdoms were Alemanni, Anglo-Saxons, Franks, Burgundians, Visigoths, Suevi, Ostrogoths, Heruli, Lombards and Vandals.

ANGLO
SAXONS

FRANKS

LOMBARDS

BERGUNDIANS/ALEMANNI

OSTROGOTHS

SUEVI

VISIGOTHS

HERULI

VANDALS

Daniel 7:8 - The dream then shows the arrival of a special 'little horn'. It comes up from among the ten horns on the fourth beast's head. So it originates in Europe. Its emergence causes three horns to be uprooted. As a prophetic horn, it represents a ruler of some kind. Moreover, it is identified with a man; for it has eyes, and a mouth that speaks boastfully.

Here is a quotation from 'The Rise of the Mediaeval Church' by Alexander Flick:

".....out of the ruins of political Rome, arose the great moral Empire in the giant form of the Roman Church".

And, another quotation from Adolf von Harnack. 'What is Christianity':

"When the western half of the Roman Empire fell to the Germanic tribes, the Bishop of Rome became an important figure in the West, and soon he exercised not only spiritual but also political power. The Roman Church in this way pushed itself into the place of the Roman World Empire of which it is the actual continuation. The empire has not perished but has only undergone a transformation".

Did Papal Rome actually uproot three kingdoms in its rise to power? Yes it did. The following three kingdoms fought against the Roman Church's mandates, and were destroyed as a result. The Ostrogoths, Vandals and Heruli disappeared from existence.

We can confidently identify the fourth ruling empire as Political/Pagan Rome, followed by Papal Rome, represented in the dream by a horn with the eyes of a man, and a mouth that speaks boastfully. Papal Rome led by the Papacy (the church institution of leadership by a Pope) is the little horn.

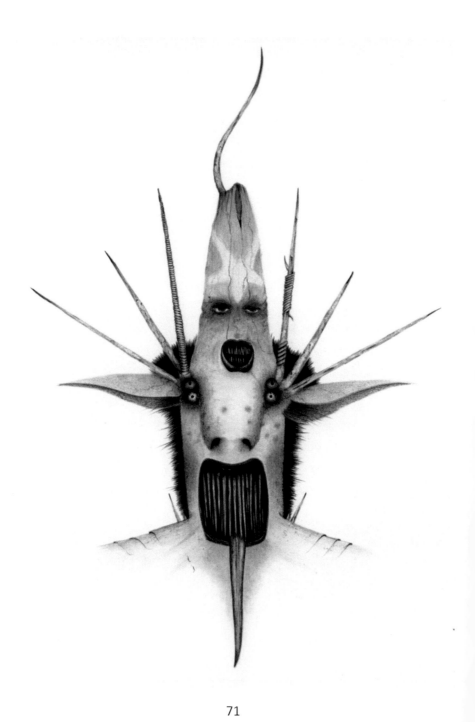

Daniel 7:9-10 – The scene in Daniel's dream changes, for while the little horn is causing havoc on earth, something important is taking place in heaven. A court room is being set up, thrones are put in place, and the Ancient of Days takes His seat. Who is the Ancient of Days?

Daniel 7:13,14 show the Son of Man being presented to the Ancient of Days. Who is the Son of Man?

When Jesus was on earth His favourite title was 'the Son of Man' (see Luke 19:10, Matthew 16:13-16). Then John 20:16,17, Hebrews 10:12, Hebrews 1:3 tell us that after Jesus had completed His work on earth, He was presented to God the Father in heaven. Therefore, in Daniel 7:13 the Ancient of Days, to whom the Son of Man (Jesus) is presented, is God the Father.

God the Father (the Ancient of Days) is described:
- His clothing is as white as snow;
- His hair is white like wool;
- His throne is flaming with fire;
- The wheels of His throne are all ablaze;
- A river of fire flows out from before Him.

An important feature of God's throne is that it has wheels; it is therefore mobile. The mobility of God's throne is significant, for, in Daniel's dream, God's throne is moved to the heavenly courtroom, which means it was previously situated elsewhere. We will explore this transporting of God's throne in our look at Daniel chapter nine. At this point, what we can say is, all activity in heaven is moved to the courtroom.

The Father takes His seat attended by thousands upon thousands, and with ten thousand times ten thousand standing before Him. Who are all these people? As this judgement begins and ends while people are living on earth, it cannot be people from earth attending Him or standing before His throne. Similarly, these people in heaven cannot be those who have died. Psalm 104:29 tells us that when we die we go back to the dust, and 1 Thessalonians 4:13-18 tell us that those who die believing in Jesus, stay in their graves until the second coming of Jesus. Revelation 20:4,5 tell us those who die without giving their hearts to Jesus stay in their graves until the Third Coming of Jesus. Therefore, humans from planet earth will not be in heaven during the judgement. (For a full explanation of the Second and Third Advents of Jesus, please see the companion to this book 'An Idiot's Guide to the Book of Revelation, chapter 20).

The attendants are most likely angels as they are the ones who attend God in heaven (See Hebrews 1:14). And, those who stand before His throne appear to be witnesses of the judgement process; seeing that justice is done. Could these be people from other inhabited planets in the universe? In 1 Corinthians 4:9 Paul writes, God's people have *"been made a spectacle to the whole universe."* So perhaps Daniel's dream shows created beings, from other planets in the universe, present at the heavenly court session.

In this court scene the books are opened. Revelation 20:11,12 tell us that each of us has a book showing our life deeds. It seems clear Daniel is viewing the judgement of every action we have carried out, as written in each person's personal book of record (see Ecclesiastes 12:14).

An appropriate name for the judgement in Daniel 7 is the Investigative Judgement, for it is an investigation of the books of God's professed people. It takes place whilst we are living on planet earth. Our books of record will be opened and our lives judged, and if found faithful, our names will be retained in the Book of Life (see Psalm 69:27,28). We will not be present at this judgement. As our books are there, our presence is unnecessary. And, fortunately, Jesus, our Mediator, Lawyer, and Defender, stands before the Father pleading our respective cases (see 1 Timothy 2:5, Hebrews 9:11,12). Of course, Jesus is only able to plead for those people He is personally acquainted with.

Revelation 20:11,12 show a different judgement, the executive judgement, which takes place 1,000 years after Jesus' second coming. As the judgement shown in Daniel 7 is for all those who profess to follow Jesus, the executive judgement is the meting out of sentences to the wicked (those who do not follow Jesus). (For information on the executive judgement please see the companion book 'An Idiot's Guide to the Book of Revelation', chapter 20).

Daniel 7:11-12 – The scene moves back to earth as we witness the actions of the little horn (the Papal Power or Papacy). He is still speaking boastful words. In fact, he continues to behave in this way until he dies and his body destroyed in the blazing fire. This fire must be the lake of fire (hell fire), also known as the Second Death, which takes place after the 1,000 years, and utterly destroys the wicked. We are told that the other beasts (the three world ruling empires) are also to be stripped of their authority, but will be allowed to live for a period of time. This period, is the time just after the end of the 1,000 years. (For a full explanation of the 1,000 years please see the companion book 'An Idiot's Guide to the Book of Revelation', chapter 20).

Just a note here. The little horn, referred to as a man speaking boastful things, symbolises the Papal institution, not a specific Pope.

Daniel 7:13-14 – Once again, we view the court judgement in heaven. Jesus, the Son of Man, is brought into the presence of His Father (the Ancient of Days). Jesus is given authority, glory and sovereign power. All nations and peoples of every language worship Him. His dominion is an everlasting dominion that will not pass away, and His kingdom is one that will never be destroyed. This scene confirms the Investigative Judgement takes place in heaven. Jesus is identified as having received all the authority, glory and honour that are rightfully His. In heaven, He is acknowledged as the victorious God with an everlasting dominion. This proclamation of the eternal power and dominion of Jesus contrasts the temporary dominion of the little horn who is boastfully wielding power on earth.

Daniel 7:15-25 – Daniel is still dreaming, but in his dream he is perturbed. He wants to understand what he is seeing. He approaches an angel and asks him to interpret the dream so far. He is especially concerned about the fourth beast, which is so destructive. He wants to know the meaning of its ten horns, and the subsequent little horn; for he now sees the little horn waging war against God's people (His saints), and defeating them. Thankfully, Daniel then sees the Investigative Judgement come to an end, and all the saints pronounced guiltless. Once this is done, then Jesus will return to earth and collect His faithful ones. The angel also assures Daniel that God's holy people will receive the kingdom and possess it forever and ever.

The angel gives Daniel the meaning of the dream, as follows:

Dream Symbol:	Angel's Interpretation:	Historical reference:
Four great beasts	Four earthly kingdoms	The four world-ruling empires: • Babylon (605BC-539BC) • Medo-Persia (539BC–331BC) • Greece (331BC-168BC) • Pagan/Political Rome (168BC-AD476)
The fourth beast's Ten Horns	Ten kingdoms that come out of the fourth world-ruling kingdom.	Following the fall of the Roman Empire, Europe was split into ten kingdoms: • Anglo Saxons • Franks • Alemanni • Lombards • Ostrogoths • Heruli • Burgundians • Visigoths • Suevi • Vandals
Little Horn that emerges and uproots three of the fourth beast's ten horns.	Another ruler (different from the rest). He will subdue three of the ten kingdoms.	The Papacy (Papal Rome) – political and religious power. The emergence of Papal Rome destroyed the Ostrogoths, Vandals and Heruli.

The angel further explains that the little horn (the Papacy) wields power against the saints of God. He speaks against the Most High, and oppresses

God's people. He will try to change the *"set times and laws"* (Daniel 7:25). As it is an angel giving the interpretation to Daniel, he must be referring to the times of God, and the law of God. The Papacy, the institution that leads the Roman Catholic Church, has indeed tried to change the set times and laws. The Catholic Church is not bashful in proclaiming its authority to change the law of God - the Ten Commandments.

When comparing the list of Ten Commandments in the Catholic Catechism to the Bible's list in Exodus 20:1-17, we find some significant differences. The Ten Commandments were proclaimed by God to the Children of Israel at Mount Sinai. He then wrote them with His own finger on tables of stone (indicating their permanency), which He handed to Moses. Moses recorded them in Exodus 20, and they have remained in the Bible for mankind to read and understand. Jesus, when on earth, told his disciples that He will never change one letter, nor one stroke of a pen of the law (see Matthew 5:17-19). Yet, the Catholic Church has sought to make substantial changes. The second commandment, shown in Exodus 20:4-6, is missing from the Catholic Catechism. This commandment, which prohibits the bowing down to any graven image or idol, has been completely removed. As one of the Catholic Church's practices is to pray to statues of Jesus, Mary, the apostles, and those designated as saints, we can understand why the Church would seek to delete the commandment that forbids this practice.

Because (in the Catechism) the second commandment has been erased, the numbering of the remaining commandments is altered. The third commandment becomes the second, the fourth commandment becomes the third, and so on.

The original fourth commandment (now the third) also poses a problem for the Catholic Church because it reminds us to keep holy the seventh-day Sabbath (Saturday). The Sabbath is a memorial of God's creation of heaven and earth in six days. He rested on the first Sabbath (the seventh day of creation week), blessed it and made it holy, and instructs us to rest from our work and worship Him on that day every week (see Exodus 20:8-11). The Catholic Church makes no secret of its attempt to change God's day of worship from the seventh day (Saturday) to Sunday, the first day of the week. The Church freely admits there is no scriptural instruction for this action.

Some Christian churches maintain that the Sabbath was given only to the Jews. However, as God instituted the Sabbath at creation, before the Jewish nation existed, this argument cannot be sustained. Moreover, as the Catholic church clearly states that it has changed the Christian Sabbath from Saturday to Sunday for its own purpose, and without God's permission, it is clear that all churches choosing to worship on Sunday, are following a Papal decree.

Please see the following three quotations from Catholic sources:

Stephen Keenan, A Doctrinal Catechism - 3rd edition, page 174.

"Question: Have you any other way of proving that the Church has power to institute festivals of precept?

"Answer: Had she not such power, she could not have done that in which all modern religionists agree with her - she could not have substituted the observance of Sunday, the first day of the week, for the observance of Saturday, the seventh day, a change for which there is no Scriptural authority."

Catholic Virginian October 3, 1947, page 9, article. "To Tell You the Truth."

"For example, nowhere in the Bible do we find that Christ or the Apostles ordered that the Sabbath be changed from Saturday to Sunday. We have the commandment of God given to Moses to keep holy the Sabbath day, that is the 7th day of the week, Saturday. Today most Christians keep Sunday because it has been revealed to us by the [Roman Catholic] church outside the Bible."

Peter Geiermann. The Converts Catechism of Catholic Doctrine. (1957 edition), page 50.

"Question: Which is the Sabbath day?

"Answer: Saturday is the Sabbath day.

"Question: Why do we observe Sunday instead of Saturday?

"Answer: We observe Sunday instead of Saturday because the Catholic Church transferred the solemnity from Saturday to Sunday."

By its own admission the Catholic Church sought to change the set times, by altering the day of worship, and the set laws by deleting one of the Ten Commandments.

The Catholic Church claims authority to change God's law. By removing the second, and changing the fourth, it now only has nine commandments in its list. This problem is addressed by dividing the tenth commandment, which prohibits coveting anything that belongs to others (see Exodus 20:17). So now the Catholic Catechism reads:

- Commandment number 9 – *"You shall not covet your neighbour's wife."*

- Commandment number 10 – *"You shall not covet your neighbour's goods."*

Problem solved. This is definitely the little horn speaking boastfully against the Most High. The Church of Rome believes it is powerful enough to change God's law, and the time designated to worship Him. This is what God says in Psalms 89:34 *"I will not violate my covenant or alter what my lips have uttered."* God spoke the Ten Commandments from Mount Sinai, and He states, He will not alter what He has said. However, the Catholic Church feels empowered to alter God's word.

In Daniel 7:25 the angel goes on. God's holy people will be delivered into the hands of the little horn for a period of time. This period of persecution for the saints of God is portrayed in various parts of the Bible, and written in various forms, as follows:-
- Time, times and half a time (Daniel 7:25)
- Time, times and half a time (Daniel 12:7)
- 42 months (Revelation 11:2)
- 1,260 days (Revelation 11:3)
- 1,260 days (Revelation 12:6)
- Time, times and half a time (Revelation 12:14)
- 42 months (Revelation 13:5)

As this time period is given as part of prophecy, the rule of prophetic time applies. We must calculate it using the 'day/year principle' outlined in Ezekiel 4:6 and Numbers 14:34 when God instructed His prophets to use one day to equal one year when deciphering prophecy time periods. The principle is:

one prophetic day equals one literal year.

The above prophetic time periods all make sense if the day/year principle is used. There are numerous time periods given in Bible prophecies dealing with earth's events. Unless indicated otherwise, the day/year principle can be used for all of them.

Using the day/year principle for the time period in Daniel's dream: **time, times and half a time**, we can calculate the period as follows:

- Time   = 1 year
- Times   = 2 years
- Half a Time   = half a year (6 months)

As the ancient Jewish/Hebrew calendar, known as the Biblical Lunar Calendar (BLC) governs all Bible chronology, it stands to reason that prophetic time will use the same calendar.

In the ancient Jewish calendar, each of its 12 months is made up of 30 days. Therefore, one prophetic year equals 360 prophetic days (12 x 30 = 360).

Here are the various Bible prophetic time periods concerning the Roman Catholic Church's era of supremacy and persecution. When calculated using the day/year principle, each period equals 1,260 years:

Time period 3.1/2 times, as shown in: Daniel 7:25, Daniel 12:7, Revelation 12:14	Time period converted to prophetic time	Prophetic time converted to prophetic days	Application of day/year principle: 1 prophetic day = 1 literal year
Time	= 1 year	= 360 prophetic days *(12 months x 30 days)*	= 360 literal years
Times	= 2 years	= 720 prophetic days *(24 months x 30 days)*	= 720 literal years
Half a time	= 6 months	= 180 prophetic days *(6 months x 30 days)*	= 180 literal years
Total			**1,260 literal years**

OR

Prophetic time as shown in: Revelation 11:2, Revelation 13:5	Time period converted to prophetic days	Time period calculated as prophetic days	Application of day/year principle: 1 prophetic day = 1 literal year
42 months	= 42 x 30 days	= 1,260 prophetic days	= 1,260 literal years

OR

Prophetic time as shown in: Revelation 11:3, Revelation 12:6	Application of day/year principle: 1 prophetic day = 1 literal year
1,260 prophetic days	= 1,260 literal years

(The day/year principle is also proved in another Bible prophecy called 'the 2,300 days' found in Daniel 9:24-27. We will examine this prophecy in Chapter 9 of this book.)

In Daniel 7:25 Daniel dreamed God's people would suffer at the hands of the little horn for 1,260 literal years. Therefore, the question we must ask at this point is, can this prophecy be substantiated by history?

Here is a quote from 'Truth Matters'. Professor Walter J Veith:
"The legally recognized supremacy of the Pope began in 538 AD, when Emperor Justinian elevated the Bishop of Rome to the position of Head of all Churches. This is known as the Edict of Justinian. Adding 1260 years to 538 AD brings us to 1798, which is the year the Pope was deposed when the French General Berthier, under Napoleon, led him into captivity. Napoleon apparently tried to crush the Papacy, and about 18 months later the Pope died in exile in Valence, France. This act ended papal power in terms of enforcing papal decrees."

The 1,260 years between AD538 and 1798 is an infamous period in European history known as the Dark Ages. It is the time when the Catholic Church carried out the most brutal persecution of anyone not adhering to the dictates of the Roman Catholic Church. This oppression included Christian martyrs burned at the stake; the Spanish Inquisition; the reign of Mary 1 of England; the Crusades; and many more dark periods in history when all those refusing to bow to the Catholic Church were tortured and/or horrifically murdered. Daniel recorded the exact time of this bloody tyranny a thousand years before it happened.

Daniel 7:26-27 – The angel ends his interpretation on an encouraging note. Whilst the Papacy is at the height of its power, from AD538 to 1798, God does not stand idly by. He promises the heavenly court will be convened. And, the end of the great controversy will be decided. God wins! The power of the little horn will be taken away and completely destroyed forever.

"Then the sovereignty, power and greatness
of all the kingdoms under heaven
will be handed over to the holy people
of the Most High.
His kingdom will be an everlasting kingdom,
and all rulers will worship and obey Him."

For God's people living on earth now, our task is to stay on the winning side. The Investigative Judgement has been going on in heaven for a while now. God has been looking through the record books of each person who has professed to be His follower. Remember, whenever your book comes up for scrutiny you will not be there, and you will not know. Your book will speak for you. It is our duty to live a life dedicated to God, so that whenever He opens our book Jesus can stand and say 'Yes he (or she) is a sinner but by faith they have accepted My sacrifice on their behalf. They are covered by My Blood!'

Bear in mind that if you are not a professed follower of Jesus, you cannot be included in the Investigative Judgement, and therefore be eligible for salvation and eternal life. But, to be included is an easy matter. All that is required is a prayer admitting you are a sinner, and requesting that God save you. He will take it from there, and let you know what to do next.

Daniel 7:28 – Daniel's dream has ended, but he is still perplexed. What he has seen is swimming around in his head and he cannot make sense of it. His thoughts are troubled, his face is pale, but he keeps everything to himself.

Footnote:

"We also have the prophetic message as something completely reliable, and you will do well to pay attention to it, as to a light shining in a dark place, until the day dawns and the morning star rises in your hearts. Above all, you must understand that no prophecy of Scripture came about by the prophet's own interpretation of things. For prophecy never had its origin in the human will, but prophets, though human, spoke from God as they were carried along by the Holy Spirit." (2 Peter 1:19-21)

We can trust the Bible. It reveals what will happen in the future. Most of Daniel 7 has already taken place exactly as Daniel's dream predicted. All that is left is the conclusion of the Investigative Judgement; the Second Coming of Jesus; the saints of God receiving the eternal kingdom; and the destruction of the little horn power. Because the prophecy has been fulfilled to the letter so far, we can be fully confident that the remainder will also take place, to the letter. The Bible is true.

Daniel Chapter Eight

A CHARGING RAM AND RAGING GOAT

Based on Daniel 8:1-27

Two years after his dream, recorded in Daniel chapter seven, Daniel has a second vision, and is greatly perplexed because he cannot understand what it means. While he is pondering, the angel Gabriel arrives to give him the vision's interpretation. This makes it easy for us; we don't have to work out the vision's meaning, we can simply compare it with history to see whether it has been fulfilled.

Incidentally, from now on in the book of Daniel, Gabriel becomes a frequent visitor and a real support to Daniel. He takes on the role of vision interpreter, helping Daniel understand the God-given revelations, and advising and comforting Daniel as he becomes more and more distressed.

This is the vision of Daniel chapter eight:

Daniel 8:1 – Daniel receives his second vision during the third year of Belshazzar's reign. As we know, Belshazzar is king Nebuchadnezzar's grandson, and the king who saw the writing on the wall in Daniel chapter five. Therefore, at this time, the kingdom of Babylon is still in power.

Daniel 8:2-4 – In his vision, Daniel sees himself standing by the Ulai Canal in the city of Susa, part of the ancient Elamite Empire (now Shusha in Iran). He looks up, and sees a ram with two long horns. After a time, one of the horns grows longer than the other. The ram is angry and charges towards the west, north and south. No animal can defeat it, nor rescue others from its power; it does as it pleases, and becomes great.

Daniel 8:5-8 – As Daniel thinks about the ram, suddenly a goat appears from the west. It has a prominent horn between its eyes. It is travelling so fast over the whole earth its feet do not touch the ground. There is a showdown between the goat and the ram, but the ram is powerless. The goat furiously attacks the ram, and breaks its two horns. It knocks the ram to the ground, and tramples on it. The goat then begins to grow in power, but at the height of its reign its prominent horn is broken off and replaced by four horns that point towards the four winds of heaven, or four compass points – north, south, east and west.

Daniel 8:9-12 – Then, from out of one of the four compass points appears an individual horn, which starts small but grows in size and power. It expands towards the south, east and toward *"the Beautiful Land"*. We can safely assume that to Daniel 'the Beautiful Land' would have been Judea, his homeland. The horn also grows in height, even as far as the stars of heaven, and proceeds to throw some of the stars down to the earth, and trample on them. It goes on to set itself up in opposition to the commander of the Lord's army. It takes away *"the daily"* and throws down the Lord's sanctuary. Through rebellion, the Lord's people and *"the daily"* are given over to the horn's dominion (we will look at the term *"the daily"* below). The horn prospers, and consequently truth is thrown to the ground.

Daniel 8:13-14 – Daniel then overhears a conversation between two angels. One is asking the other how long will the detestable actions, carried out by the new horn, last. The second angel then turns to Daniel and gives him the answer. He says *"It will take 2,300 days; then the sanctuary will be reconsecrated"* (or cleansed). Daniel 8:14, which introduces the 2,300 day period is a prophecy in itself. We will look at this prophecy in the next two chapters.

Daniel 8:15-19 – Gabriel comes to the rescue. Daniel, greatly disturbed by his vision, needs someone to calm him. Therefore, God sends Gabriel - one of His mightiest angels. In the New Testament, it was Gabriel who revealed to Zechariah that his wife would have a son (John the Baptist). Gabriel introduced himself to Zechariah as, one who stands in the presence of God (see Luke 1:19). We can therefore trust Gabriel, for he receives instruction direct from God.

Daniel is terrified at the sight of Gabriel, and faints. Gabriel revives him, and reassures him that he has come to give him the vision's interpretation. However, he warns Daniel the vision is not for his time, but will extend to the time of the end.

Daniel 8:20-25 – We often see beasts in Bible prophecy. Daniel 7:17 tells us prophetic beasts symbolise earthly nations. And, Revelation 17:12 states that horns on prophetic beasts signify individual kings or kingdoms.

Gabriel tells Daniel, the two-horned ram represents the allied nation of Media and Persia. Persia became the more powerful nation of this alliance, thus explaining why one of the ram's horns grew longer than the other. Once again, we are viewing the world ruling empires. This is the third time we have encountered this allied power. You will notice Babylon, which ruled before Medo-Persia, is not included in this vision. God is homing in on Nebuchadnezzar's dream of Daniel 2, this time, beginning with the second empire, as Babylon is soon to be overthrown by the Persians.

With the revelation that Medo-Persia is the ram, we already know the kingdom that overthrows it is Greece. And, true enough, Gabriel confirms the raging goat represents Greece. Its long horn is the Grecian Empire's king, whom we know is Alexander the Great. We also know, from the Daniel 7 dream, that following Alexander's premature death, four Greek army generals succeeded him but, as Gabriel now says, they cannot wield the same power as Alexander. In the latter part of the generals' reign *"a fierce-looking king, a master of intrigue will arise"* (Daniel 8:23). This is the horn that comes out of one of the four compass points, signifying the emergence of a new ruler. The horn will become very strong, but not by his own power; he receives his power and strength from someone else.

The horn power of Daniel 8 (in its early stage) is the same as the fourth beast of Daniel 7. It is the power of Rome that came out of the west to overthrow the Greek Empire. As we have already learned, Rome appeared as a Pagan power, but then, under the rulership of Emperor Constantine, Papal Rome began to emerge wielding both political and religious power. This fusion of church and state gave the horn power (now Papal Rome) its great strength to figuratively reach up to heaven, for it opposed the teachings of the Bible, sought to change the law of God, attacked the ministration of Jesus in the heavenly sanctuary, and, labelled as the *"abomination that causes desolation"* (see Daniel 9:27), caused the terrible oppression of God's people.

Gabriel's statement that the horn *"will become very strong, but not by his own power"* (Daniel 8:24), gives insight into the part played by Emperor Constantine in bringing the Roman Catholic Church to a position of power and great influence within his government. As a convert to the church, Constantine passed laws instituting Catholicism as the state religion and commanding his subjects to adopt the Catholic faith.

The Roman Papal power also appears in the prophecies of the book of Revelation. In Revelation 13 a leopard-like beast is described, which becomes the personification of the Papacy. Revelation 13:2 makes it clear the leopard-like beast receives its power and authority from the devil himself. Could it be that in Daniel 8, Gabriel's description of the Papacy becoming strong *"but not by his own power"* (Daniel 8:24) is also a warning that the Papacy is an agent of the devil? This is a serious indictment, but when we see the actions of the horn power, we must conclude its power does not originate from God. Daniel 8:10 tells us *"it reached the host of the heavens, and ….. threw some of the starry host down to the earth and trampled on them."* We can compare this verse with Daniel 8:13 which tells us this apostate religious power will trample God's people underfoot. The trampling of the starry host and the trampling of God's people appear to be the same action. In Revelation chapter one, the leaders of God's church are described as stars, and in Revelation 2, the courageous Protestant reformers (14th-16th centuries) are called the *"morning star"*. Therefore, the trampling of the starry host could well refer to the persecution of prominent followers of God by the Roman Catholic Church.

A further link between the horn power (the Catholic Church) and the devil is the fact that they behave similarly. The devil, portrayed as the great red dragon in Revelation 12, sweeps one-third of the stars of heaven out of the sky and flings them to earth (see Revelation 12:4), thus mirroring the actions of the horn of Daniel 8 which we are told *"threw some of the starry host down to the earth..."* (Daniel 8:10).

As with the little horn of Daniel 7, the horn of Daniel 8 is referred to as *"he"*. This indicates that both horns are spearheaded by a male ruler. The Daniel 8 horn is described as causing *"astounding devastation"*, destroying the holy people, and even standing against the *"Prince of princes"* (Daniel 8:24,25). It seems clear that the title 'Prince of princes' refers to Jesus, as Gabriel will call Him the *"great prince"* later in Daniel (Daniel 12:1). Therefore, the horn will have the audacity to oppose Jesus (His teachings, ministry, and followers). This horn power is so strong it will take the supernatural power of God to destroy it.

Further confirmation that the little horn (Daniel 7), the horn (Daniel 8), and the leopard-like beast (Revelation 13) are one and the same – the Roman Papal power/Catholic Church – is shown in the fact that all three come to power after Pagan Rome and display the same blasphemous behaviour, as shown in the following chart:

Actions of the Little Horn of Daniel 7:	Actions of the Horn of Daniel 8:	Actions of the leopard-like beast of Revelation 13:
• The horn has a human mouth that speaks boastfully; • It will speak against the Most High; • It will try to change the set times and laws; • It will oppress God's holy people; • It wages war against the holy people and defeats them; • The holy people will be delivered into his hands for a time, times and half a time (1,260 years).	• It grew until it reached the host of the heavens; • It set itself up to be as great as Jesus; • It throws the sanctuary down; • It attacks God's people, and destroys them, trampling them underfoot; • It throws truth to the ground; • It will cause astounding devastation; • It will cause deceit to prosper; • It will consider itself superior; • It will destroy many.	• It is given a mouth to utter proud words; • It blasphemes (speaks against God); • It slanders God's name; • It slanders God's dwelling place; • It slanders those who live in heaven; • It is given power to wage war against God's holy people and conquer them; • It exercises its authority for 42 months (1,260 years); • It is given authority over the whole world.

Just a note here regarding references to *"the daily"* in Daniel 8:12,13. Some Bible translators add the word 'sacrifice' to the phrase, so it reads *"...it (the horn) took away the daily sacrifice"*. No doubt, the translators did this in an effort to explain the meaning of 'the daily'. This well-meaning addition thus implies the rampaging Papacy will destroy the daily sacrifices performed by the Jews. However, as it was the death of Jesus on the cross (the true sacrifice for sin) that did away with the daily sacrificial system. We must look elsewhere for the meaning of the horn taking away 'the daily'.

Joshua Himes in 'The Second Advent Manual' page 66, commenting on William Miller's study of Daniel 8, states that Miller compared Daniel 8:12,13 with 2 Thessalonians 2:7,8, as both talk about the Papacy taking something *"out of the way"*. Miller concluded that both the Apostle Paul, and Daniel, are referring to the same event; namely, the Roman Papal power overtaking the Roman Pagan power. Pagan Rome ruled in the time of Paul. Thus, it was the ruler of the day (the daily). Moreover, in 2 Thessalonians 2:7,8, Paul (like

Daniel) prophesies that Pagan Rome will be superseded by Papal Rome, whom he refers to as *"the power of lawlessness"*: an interesting title, as it is the Roman Catholic Church that sought to change God's law.

History also sheds light on the emergence of Catholicism. For, Emperor Constantine's first edict of AD324 stated the Roman Catholic Church (the Christian church at that time) was to be embraced by his subjects, and replace Paganism.
(www.nationalgeographic.com/culture/people/reference/constantine)

It appears, then, that when Daniel 8:12,13 refers to the horn taking away *"the daily"* it is making a distinction between Pagan Rome and Papal Rome; stating that Papal Rome will supersede Pagan Rome.

Daniel 8:26-27 – Gabriel then refers to Daniel 8:13,14 which speak about the cleansing of the sanctuary. He says this prophecy is true, but it *"concerns the distant future"*. Therefore, he instructs Daniel to *"seal up the vision"*. In other words, Daniel's God-given role was to record the vision, but not worry about its fulfilment, as this would not come until the time of the end (our time). Easier said than done. Daniel is worn out; he stays in bed for several days after this experience. And, when he is once again able to resume his court duties, he finds himself pre-occupied, for he is pondering over what he has seen.

Daniel Chapter Eight (verse Fourteen)
DAY OF ATONEMENT (The Cleansing of the Sanctuary)

Based on Daniel 8:14, Exodus 25-30, Leviticus 16

Daniel 8:14 speaks about the cleansing of the sanctuary. It says, '….it will take 2,300 days, then the sanctuary will be cleansed.' In order for us to grasp the meaning of this verse, we must first look at the Jewish sanctuary services and how the earthly sanctuary was cleansed.

While the Children of Israel were journeying through the wilderness, after being rescued from slavery in Egypt, God instructed them to build a sanctuary, which was a structure designed to enable them to approach Him in worship (see Exodus 25:8). The structure could be erected, dismantled and transported. And, wherever the people camped, the structure was set up. The sanctuary had a courtyard, and within the courtyard was a tent called the tent of meeting or tabernacle.

Among the sanctuary furniture were two altars; the altar of burnt offering, situated in the sanctuary courtyard, and the altar of incense, situated in the tent of meeting's first compartment called the Holy Place. Both altars had a hook at each of its four corners. These hooks were referred to as 'horns'. Animal sacrifices were burned on the altar of burnt offering. And incense, representing the prayers of the people, was burned on the altar of incense.

Leviticus 4:1-7 and verses 27-35 describe the continual sin offerings overseen by the priests in the wilderness sanctuary. Throughout the year, as part of the sanctuary service, bulls, sheep and goats were killed and burned as sacrifices for the sins of the people. The people confessed their sins on the head of the animal being offered. They then killed the animal which was burned on the altar of burnt offering situated in the sanctuary's courtyard. The priest wiped some of the animal's blood on the horns of the altar, and the remainder was poured at the altar's base.

For sin offerings for the priests, the blood of the animal was also carried into the Holy Place, or first compartment of the tent of meeting, and sprinkled seven times in front of the curtain that separated the Holy Place from the second compartment called the Most Holy Place, or Holy of Holies. The priests also wiped some of the blood of this sacrifice on the horns of the altar of incense, in the first compartment, and the remainder was poured at the base of the altar of burnt offering. The sin offering symbolised the death of the true sacrifice for our sins, Jesus Christ, through which mankind is cleansed from sin. The sanctuary service was always intended to be a symbol of the real sacrifice to come.

The blood of these daily sacrifices, figuratively carried the confessed sins of the people into the sanctuary. This meant the sanctuary was constantly being defiled, or desecrated, by sin, and would at some point require cleansing.

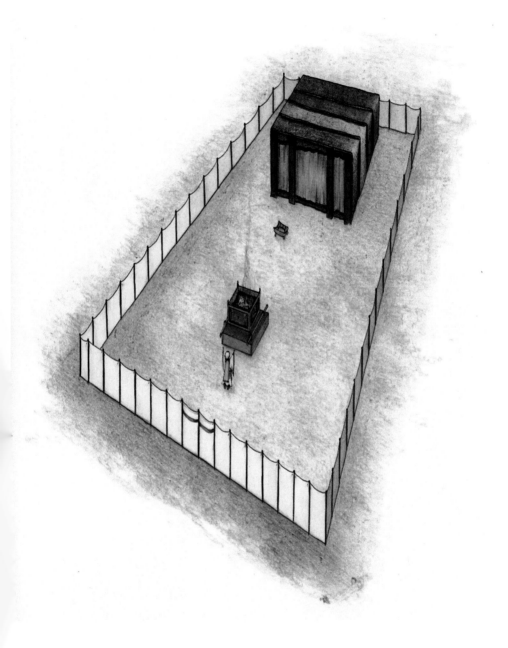

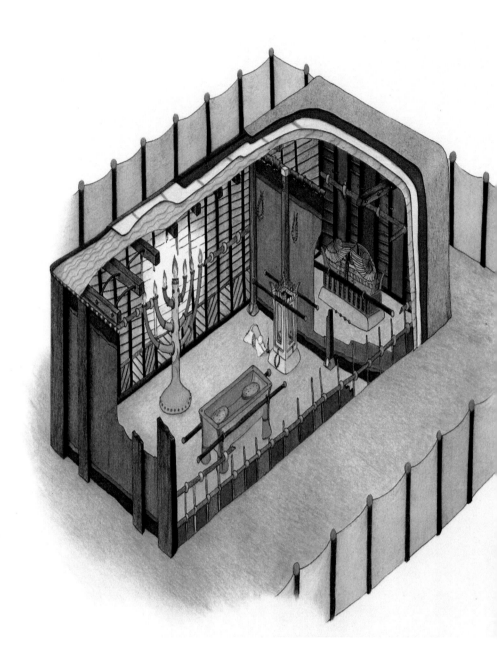

'Day of Atonement' was the name given to the annual ceremony that symbolised the cleansing of the sanctuary from all the accumulated sins of the people over the year. Leviticus 16:11-14 tell of the preliminary part of the ceremony, namely, the sacrificing of a bull for the High Priest, who had to be cleansed of sin in order to qualify him to carry out his part in the annual service.

Leviticus 16:15-19 describe the sanctuary cleansing ceremony, commencing with the choosing of two goats. One was designated the Lord's goat, the other, the scapegoat. The Lord's goat was killed, and the High Priest carried its blood into the Most Holy Place, the second compartment of the sanctuary behind the curtain. In this compartment stood the Ark of the Covenant (a chest which held the Ten Commandments written on two stone tablets by the finger of God). The cover of the Ark of the Covenant was called the Mercy Seat, and the High Priest sprinkled the goat's blood both on this cover, and in front of the chest. The Ark of the Covenant with the Ten Commandments and the Mercy Seat represented the throne of God; for His government is founded on His law, yet justice is administered through His mercy and grace.

On his way out of the sanctuary, the High Priest sprinkled the goat's blood on the altar of incense and its horns. Thus, the sanctuary was cleansed of the confessed sins of the people accumulated throughout the year. The sins, now figuratively transferred onto the person of the High Priest, were carried out of the sanctuary.

Leviticus 16:20-22 show what happened to the scapegoat. The High Priest confessed all the sins of the people, now cleansed from the sanctuary, onto the head of the scapegoat. Then a strong man was chosen to lead this goat into a remote and uninhabited desert region, where it was left to die.

The Lord's goat represents Jesus; the Lamb of God, who takes away the sin of the world. His death at Calvary paid the required price for all our sins (see John 1:29, Hebrews 9:11-15, Romans 6:23).

The scapegoat represents the devil who will finally bear the confessed sins of God's people, and be destroyed in the lake of fire (hell fire) (see Revelation 20:1-3, 7-10).

All the earthly sanctuary services pointed to the real ministry of Jesus. Therefore, the annual cleansing of the Jewish sanctuary (Day of Atonement) served as a type, or illustration, of the cleansing of the true sanctuary situated in heaven (see Hebrews 8:1,2).

Exodus 25-30 list the meticulous instructions given by God to Moses regarding the building of the earthly sanctuary, together with the making of its furniture and service utensils. In Exodus 25:40 God says *"See that you make them according to the pattern shown you on the mountain."* Hebrews 8:1-6 further explains that the sanctuary on earth was merely a copy, or pattern, of the real sanctuary in heaven, where Jesus is both our High Priest, and Sacrifice for sin (see Hebrews 10:10-14, Hebrews 9:11-15, 23-28).

In Daniel chapter eight, Gabriel warns Daniel that the cleansing of the sanctuary, referred to in his vision, is set in the distant future, or the time of the end (see Daniel 8:19,26). This means the prophecy, which begins with the statement in Daniel 8:14 *"It will take 2,300 days, then the sanctuary will be reconsecrated"* (cleansed), cannot be referring to the Old Testament sanctuary; Solomon's Temple; or the Temple of Jesus' time. None of these structures, in which the sacrificial services were carried out, have survived to the time of the end. Moreover, as Hebrews 9:11-14 tell us, Jesus' death at Calvary (the true sacrifice for sin) brought to an end the earthly sacrificial system. Therefore, the cleansing of the sanctuary in Daniel 8:14 must refer to the cleansing of the heavenly sanctuary.

Daniel 7:25,26 indicate that the Investigative Judgement (the judgement of God's people) takes place after the 1,260 years (the Dark Ages), when the Papacy, at the height of its supremacy, oppresses the people of God. Daniel

8:13,14 show the same sequence of events; the horn power (the Papacy), again at its strongest, persecutes the saints of God, then, the sanctuary is cleansed. Thus, the Investigative Judgement and the cleansing of the sanctuary must be the same event. This is the time when the heavenly High Priest (Jesus) enters the Holy of Holies before the throne of God (see Daniel 7:13), and the work of judgement begins, as Jesus pleads His blood for those who are covered with His righteousness. The courtroom session of Daniel 7 depicts the Investigative Judgement which is the cleansing of the heavenly sanctuary.

In the earthly cleansing ceremony, the High Priest carried the blood of the Lord's goat (representing Jesus' blood) before the Mercy Seat (symbolic of the throne of God), in order to cleanse the sanctuary of the confessed sins of the people. In the heavenly ceremony Jesus, both our High Priest and Sacrifice, stands before His Father (the Ancient of Days), and pleads His blood for those people who have confessed their sins, and are living holy lives by the grace of God. Their confessed sins are then cleared (finally blotted out), because Jesus has paid the penalty of death for them when He was crucified at Calvary (see Hebrews 9:23-26). God orders that their names be retained in the Book of Life, and they are therefore pronounced innocent (see Psalm 69:27-28, Daniel 7:22). This is how the heavenly sanctuary is cleansed. The confessed sins are assigned to the devil, and he will suffer the punishment for these sins in the lake of fire. Revelation 20 tells us that anyone thrown into the lake of fire suffers the Second Death and is utterly destroyed. (For a full explanation of the Second Death please see the companion book 'An Idiot's Guide to the Book of Revelation', chapter 20)

The earthly Day of Atonement was a very serious day for the Children of Israel. All sins needed to be confessed so they could be cleansed from the sanctuary (see Leviticus 16:29,30). In fact, whilst the High Priest was in the Most Holy Place before the Mercy Seat, the people would wait anxiously outside, reviewing their actions over the past year, for only confessed sin could be placed by the High Priest onto the head of the scapegoat, and finally destroyed. Unconfessed sin could not be included in the ceremony, as they remained with the perpetrator. Should the High Priest enter the Most Holy Place bearing unconfessed sin of his own, he would immediately be struck dead, for the presence of God automatically destroys sin (see Psalm 5:4,5). It was therefore imperative that all sins be confessed; unconfessed sins cost the High Priest his life.

As only the High Priest could enter the Most Holy Place (and only on the Day of Atonement), he would wear bells on the hem of his robe, so the people could hear him moving about in the Holy of Holies. An uncorroborated story is told of a rope being tied around the High Priest's waist so that if the bells fell silent, his body could be pulled out of the Most Holy Place.

Today, like the Children of Israel, all who profess to be Christians, are figuratively standing outside the sanctuary, making sure their sins are confessed and covered by the blood of Jesus. To confess their sins, they no longer have to sacrifice an animal. All they need do is ask God to forgive them for the sins they have committed. This confession of sin must take place each day of their lives. It enables God to forgive them and cover them with the perfect character of Jesus (see 1 John 1:9). They are then fit for heaven. This process is called 'righteousness by faith' and is the pathway to being saved and receiving eternal life (see Ephesians 2:8,9). It is open to everyone and anyone who chooses it.

Those who profess to be God's children but do not continually, and sincerely, confess their sins, cannot be pronounced innocent in the Investigative Judgement. They must bear their own sins, for unconfessed sin cannot be placed on the head of the scapegoat (the devil). These people will ultimately be thrown into the lake of fire to be destroyed with their sins (see Revelation 20:15).

What about those who do not profess to be Christians? Those who have not chosen to be covered by the blood of Jesus cannot be included in the Investigative Judgement; for Jesus cannot plead His sacrifice for those who do not acknowledge His death for their sins. Unfortunately, those who choose not to be saved will be assigned a place in the lake of fire (see Revelation 20:14,15). There is really no need for anyone to be destroyed in hell fire. A simple choice to ask God to forgive us of our misdeeds, and accept us as His children and followers of Jesus, is enough to keep us all out of the fire of final destruction.

Footnote:

The following chart compares the dreams of Daniel 2, Daniel 7 and Daniel 8.

Daniel 2 - Statue	Daniel 7 - Beasts	Daniel 8 - Beasts
Head of Gold - Babylon	Lion - Babylon	No Babylon symbol
Chest and arms - Medo-Persia	Bear - Medo-Persia	Ram - Medo-Persia
Belly and Thighs - Greece	Leopard - Greece	Goat - Greece
Legs - Political/Pagan Rome	Terrible Beast - Political/Pagan Rome	Horn starting small - Political/Pagan Rome
Legs - Papal Rome	Little Horn - Papal Rome	Horn grown large - Papal Rome
	Investigative Judgement	Cleansing of the heavenly sanctuary
Stone cut out without hands - Jesus' second coming	Saints gain the kingdom - Jesus' second coming	The small/large horn destroyed by supernatural power - Jesus' second coming

As we move to Daniel 9, we will concentrate on the 2,300 days of Daniel 8:14. From this prophecy we will learn when this prophetic time period started; when the Investigative Judgement (cleansing of the heavenly sanctuary) begins; and why these dates are relevant to us today.

Daniel Chapter Nine

THE 2,300 DAYS PROPHECY

Based on Daniel 9:1-27

In Daniel 8 we learned the horn, that started small (Pagan Rome), but grew large (Papal Rome), would attack God's people, throw down the heavenly sanctuary ministration, and stand in opposition to Jesus.

In Daniel 7 we learned the same horn power would seek to change the law of God, and speak against the Most High God. The Roman Catholic Church, whilst claiming to be a Christian church that believes in Jesus as the Saviour of the world, is nevertheless guilty of all the violations described in Daniel 7 and 8. Firstly, it is the Catholic Church that proudly boasts of having the authority to change the Ten Commandments by erasing the second of its precepts, and transferring solemnity from the seventh-day Sabbath (Saturday) to Sunday, contrary to Biblical instruction. Secondly, the Catholic Church persecuted, and put to death, millions who defied its dictates during the Dark Ages (AD538 - 1798). Thirdly, this Church continues much of the Jewish sanctuary sacrificial rituals in its services, such as the use of incense and altars, which were done away with when Christ died on the cross (see Hebrews 8:23-28). By continuing to use items from the old system of worship, Roman Catholics effectively deny the once-for-all sacrifice of Jesus. Fourthly, the Catholic Church practices the confession of sins to men (priests), which is not supported by the Bible. God's Word instructs us to confess our sins to God alone, for only He can forgive our misdemeanours (see Matthew 6:12, I John 1:9). Because of Jesus' sacrifice for us, God forgives the sins we confess to Him (see 1 John 2:1,2). Therefore, to put a man in the place of God is blasphemy and a denial of the sacrifice of Jesus. Forgiveness of sins takes place only within the domain of the Divine (see Mark 2:7).

Rome's fight against the followers of Jesus reached a pivotal point when the political/pagan Roman Empire besieged Jerusalem and destroyed its temple in AD70. Papal Rome succeeded Pagan Rome and has continued waging a religious war against followers of the truth to this day. No wonder, in Daniel 8:13, one angel asks another *"How long will it take for the vision to be fulfilled – the vision concerning the daily, the rebellion that causes desolation, the surrender of the sanctuary and the trampling underfoot of the Lord's people?"* The answer to this question is given in Daniel 8:14 'It will take 2,300 days then the (heavenly) sanctuary will be cleansed'.

In Daniel 9 we examine the longest time prophecy in the Bible – a prophecy that has special significance for the Seventh-day Adventist Church.

Daniel 9:1 - We meet Daniel in the first year of the reign of Darius, king of the Medes. It is 539BC. Remember, Darius was the king who threw Daniel into the lions' den (see Daniel 6). This means ten years have passed since Daniel received the dream of the ram and the goat in Daniel 8. There are ten years between Daniel 8 and Daniel 9.

Daniel 9:2-3 - The Jews have been in exile for 66 years, and it is at this time that Daniel makes a special, and specific, petition to God. He has been studying the book of Jeremiah, and realises the time of the Jews' captivity is coming to an end. Jeremiah prophesied the captivity of Israel would last 70 years (see Jeremiah 25:11-14). Therefore, Daniel fasts and prays, dressed in sackcloth and ashes; indicating the seriousness of his prayer, and his contrition for sin.

Daniel 9:4-19 – Daniel's petition takes the form of an intercessory prayer. Daniel is praying not only for himself, but also on behalf of the entire Jewish nation.

Here is Daniel's prayer:-

- **Verse 4** – Daniel acknowledges God as great and awesome. He confirms that God keeps His covenant of love with those who love and obey Him. In other words, God is faithful.
- **Verses 5-6** – We have sinned and done wrong. We have been wicked, rebelled, turned away from Your commands and laws, and not listened to the warnings of the prophets.
- **Verse 7** – Lord, You are righteous. We are covered with shame. We have been unfaithful to You, and we understand why You allowed our captivity.
- **Verse 8** – The whole nation has sinned against You.
- **Verse 9** – The Lord our God is merciful and forgiving, even though we have rebelled against Him.
- **Verse 10** – We have not obeyed God, or His laws.
- **Verse 11** – We have transgressed God's law, turned away and refused to obey Him. Therefore, His curse is upon us and His judgements have been poured out on us.
- **Verses 12-14** – You, God, have fulfilled Your word by bringing disaster on us, yet we have still not sought Your favour nor turned back to Your truth. You are righteous but we have not obeyed You.
- **Verses 15-19** – Lord please turn away Your anger. Our sins and iniquities have made us an object of scorn to all those around us. Hear our petitions and prayers. Forgive us. Show us mercy. Please act on our behalf and do not delay, not because we are righteous, but because we bear Your name.

Daniel is confessing the sins of his countrymen in order to remove all obstacles that could possibly prevent God fulfilling His promise to end their captivity.

The prayer of Daniel reminds every human being of their true condition. We all need the grace and mercy of God, for we have no natural goodness of our own (see Romans 3:10-12, Ephesians 2:8). Daniel's prayer is an unexaggerated

111

declaration of our standing before God. The fact is, we are sinful, and righteousness is not a part of our nature. Deep down, each one of us knows we are unworthy. The closer we get to God the more we understand this. However, this realisation can crush our spirit, and so generally, we seek to convince ourselves, and others, of our good intentions, and praiseworthy deeds, which, in reality, are no more than unauthentic perceptions of our human nature. The Bible paints a different picture; Jeremiah 7:9 warns *"The heart is deceitful above all things and beyond cure………"*. And Isaiah 64:6 tells us *"All of us have become like one who is unclean, and all our righteous acts are like filthy rags……"*. Therefore, even when we do good, both our motives and actions are tainted with selfishness, and cannot reach a level acceptable to God. We need a Saviour, one who is perfect, who has never sinned. We need a Sponsor able to cover the cost of our unworthiness with His own unblemished character, thus allowing God the Father to pardon us, and view us as though we had never sinned. Isn't it wonderful that such a Saviour exists? His name is Jesus, and His sacrifice has paid the price for the sin of the entire world (see John 3:16,17, Romans 6:23); no-one is excluded.

Daniel 9:20-23 - reveal how long it takes an angel to fly from heaven to earth. In verse 23 Gabriel tells Daniel *"As soon as you began to pray, a word went out, which I have come to tell you…….."*. From the moment Daniel began his intercessory prayer, the angel Gabriel was despatched from heaven to give an answer to his question regarding the end of the exile of the Jews. Daniel's prayer takes 2 minutes 55 seconds to recite. Moreover, we are told Gabriel set off *"in swift flight"* (Daniel 9:21) as soon as Daniel started praying, and arrived before the prayer was finished. Therefore, the time Gabriel took to fly from heaven to earth was less than 2 minutes, 55 seconds. That sounds fast to me! Does God delay in answering our prayers? This episode would suggest not. It confirms God's promise to His people in Isaiah 65:24 *"Before they call I will answer; while they are still speaking I will hear."*

In Daniel 9:23, before Gabriel answers Daniel's petition, he addresses him as "..........highly esteemed". What a revelation: human beings, although tainted by sin, can be highly regarded by the holy beings in heaven. No doubt, the 'highly esteemed' are true followers of Jesus who, like Daniel, love, trust and follow Him.

Gabriel proceeds to explain Daniel 8:14, which will answer Daniel's question. Gabriel has already interpreted the Daniel 8 vision of the charging ram and raging goat. However, no explanation was given of the time prophecy of Daniel 8:14 *"...It will take 2,300 days; then the sanctuary will be cleansed."* (KJV) This is the only part of the vision not clarified. Therefore, Gabriel has now come to clear up the mystery of the 2,300 days.

We already know the cleansing referred to is that of the heavenly sanctuary, and this cleansing will take the form of an investigation of the lives of the professed children of God, to see whether they are truly covered with the blood of Jesus (see chapters 8, and 8 (verse 14) of this book).

Now let us consider the longest time prophecy in the Bible.
Gabriel breaks down the 2,300 days of Daniel 8:14 and pinpoints exactly when the Investigative Judgement begins.

Daniel 9:24 – Gabriel states that the first 70 weeks of the 2,300 days are designated for the nation of Israel to finish transgression; put an end to sin; atone for wickedness; bring in everlasting righteousness, seal up vision and prophecy and anoint the Most Holy One (margin).

As we are dealing with prophecy, the rule for prophetic time applies, which is the day/year principle – one prophetic day equals one literal year. (This principle is fully explained in chapter 7). Gabriel has already warned Daniel the prophecy is not for his time but for the time of the end (see Daniel 8:17,19,26). As it is for our time, not Daniel's, then the days and weeks of this prophecy cannot be literal days and weeks. For example, 2,300 literal days equal 328.5 literal weeks, or just over six years, which would place the prophecy's fulfilment firmly within Daniel's time. So, the day/year principle must be used here. The 2,300 days is therefore referring to 2,300 literal years. The 70 weeks must also be prophetic time. Seventy prophetic weeks, when converted to days, equal 490 prophetic days (70 x 7 = 490), or 490 literal years.

Gabriel says 490 years, of the 2,300 year period, are for Israel to get itself in order; and sort out its standing with God as a nation. But, in order for us to understand when these periods will occur, we need to know the start date of the prophecy.

Daniel 9:25 - Gabriel gives the start date. **When the decree is given to rebuild Jerusalem** until the Messiah comes (is anointed/baptised) will be a period of 7 weeks (49 literal years), and 62 weeks (434 literal years). He then adds that the rebuilding of Jerusalem will be carried out in troublesome times. 49 years plus 434 years equal 483 years.

Gabriel is giving a breakdown of each period as follows:
- The 2,300 years begin with the decree to rebuild Jerusalem;
- The first 490 years, of the 2,300 years, are for the Jews;
- The 490 years are broken down into 49 years and 434 years (totalling 483 years);
- Therefore, a further 7 years are needed to make up the 490 years.

Daniel 9:27 – Gabriel does not disappoint us. Here is the final prophetic week (7 literal years). He states, the Messiah will confirm the covenant with many for one week, but in the middle of the week He will put an end to sacrifice and offering. So now, the 490 years have been fully accounted for.

Here is a table of prophetic time periods within the 2,300 days prophecy converted to literal time using the day/year principle (one prophetic day = one literal year):

Prophetic Time:	Equals		Prophetic Days:	Literal Time:
2,300 days		=	2,300 days	2,300 years
70 weeks	(70 x 7)	=	490 days	490 years
7 weeks	(7 x 7)	=	49 days	49 years
62 weeks	(62 x 7)	=	434 days	434 years
1 week (7 days)	(1 x 7)	=	7 days	7 years
1,810 days		=	1,810 days	1,810 years

In Daniel 9:25,27 Gabriel gives, not only the event that begins the prophecy (the royal decree to rebuild Jerusalem), but also a full breakdown of what will happen during the 490 years designated to the Jews. Moreover, if the first 490 years of the 2,300 year period are for the Jewish nation; to get itself right with God, then it seems logical to assume the time following the 490 years is for all nations.

Daniel 9:26 – Here is further information regarding the Messiah. Gabriel says the Messiah will be put to death.

We can now put together everything we have learned from Gabriel so far.

This prophecy covers 2,300 years, beginning from 457BC.
The first 490 years, of the 2,300 year period, are specifically for the Jewish nation. Gabriel then breaks down the 490 years into three sections:
- **49 years** at which time Jerusalem would be rebuilt;
- followed by **434 years** culminating in the baptism of Jesus (when He was anointed by the Holy Spirit [see Matthew 3:16,17]);
- and then a further **7 years** during which Jesus would be crucified, and thus put an end to the earthly sacrificial system. Jesus' death would take place

115

three and a half years into the **7 year** period. The final three and a half years of the period would see the apostolic church preaching the gospel of Jesus the Messiah, to the Jewish nation.

This brings us to the end of the 490 years. The gospel would then be opened up to the world, both Jews and Gentiles.

In case you need it, here is the same information given in a little more detail.

The prophecy's start date is the Autumn of 457BC when King Artaxerxes 1 gave the decree to rebuild Jerusalem (see Ezra 7:11-28). The rebuilding was vigorously opposed by some of the king's subjects, and so took place in troublesome times (see Ezra 4:7-16). Gabriel's explanation of the prophecy so far has already answered Daniel's question. Daniel now knows the rebuilding of Jerusalem is certain; God will fulfil His promise. The Jewish exile will end, just as predicted.

However, there is more information for Daniel to record, and so Gabriel continues. The first 490 years of the 2,300 year period are specifically given to the Jews as a nation; for them to put an end to their sin, and for the Most Holy One to be anointed.

Gabriel further breaks down the 490 years to, 49 years (during which Jerusalem will be rebuilt with streets and a trench) and the following 434 years that take us to AD27 when Jesus *"the Anointed One"* (Daniel 9:26) was baptised, and then anointed by the Holy Spirit (see Matthew 3:16,17, Acts 10:38).

Gabriel says, Jesus, the Messiah, will *"confirm a covenant with many"* (Daniel 9:27) for 7 years. Surely, this is Jesus' preaching of the kingdom of grace, that confirmed the covenant God made with His commandment keeping people in Jeremiah 31:33, when He promised He would be their God and they would be

116

His people. After three and a half years of preaching ministry, the Messiah, who is the true sacrifice for the sins of mankind, will be put to death (AD31), and thereby put an end to the earthly sacrificial system practised by the Jews (see Matthew 27:50,51). His disciples will carry on the preaching of the gospel, specifically to the Jews, for the remaining three and a half years, which will conclude the 490 years designated for the Jewish nation. This brings us to AD34 when Acts 7:54-60 and Acts 8:1 tell us that Stephen (one of the Apostolic Church leaders) was stoned, and consequently, the church suffered great persecution, and scattered throughout Judea and Samaria. Acts 8:4 says, wherever the early church members went, they preached the word. Therefore, the stoning of Stephen was the catalyst for the gospel being preached, not only to the Jews, but also to the Gentiles. Thus, the prophecy was fulfilled; the time of the Jews being the specially chosen nation to receive the favour of God ended in AD34.

Daniel 9:26-27 - We are given more information on what will happen to the Jews after AD34. In AD70, Jerusalem was overthrown and its temple destroyed by the Roman Empire. Jesus spoke of this terrible event in Matthew 24:15,16. History tells us the destruction of the temple was ordered by Emperor Titus in an extremely bloody siege which included the piling of bodies in great mounds, and rivers of blood flowing through the streets of Jerusalem. (www.christianitytoday.com)

The last sentence of Daniel 9:27 tells of the death of the one who destroys the temple. This could be the actual Emperor Titus who reigned for 26 years. There is much speculation as to the cause of his death.

According to the 'Babylonian Talmud (Tractate Gittin 56b)', "....*an insect flew into Titus's nose and picked at his brain for seven years. He noticed that the sound of a blacksmith hammering caused the ensuing pain to abate, so he paid for blacksmiths to hammer near him; however, the effect wore off and the insect resumed its gnawing. When he died they opened his skull and found the*

117

insect had grown to the size of a bird. The Talmud gives this as the cause of his death and interprets it as divine retribution for his wicked actions."

History also records that Titus was murdered by his younger brother, Domitian, with a poisoned fish. (www.ancienthistoryencyclopedia/titus)

Perhaps more in keeping with Daniel's earlier visions, the death of the one who set up the *"abomination that causes desolation"* (Daniel 9:27), could refer to the final end of the Papacy, as shown in Daniel 7:26 *"But the court will sit, and his power will be taken away and completely destroyed forever."* For, as we will learn in Daniel 11 and 12, the phrase 'abomination that causes desolation' refers to the uniting of church and state, namely the amalgamation of the Catholic Church and Roman government, leading to the oppression of all who refuse to follow Catholic dictates.

Now that we have accounted for the first 490 years of the 2,300 year period, we still have 1,810 years to the cleansing of the sanctuary (490 years plus 1,810 years equal 2,300 years). If we add 1,810 years to AD34 we come to the year 1844, and we can be very specific here, because if we look at the actual date when the decree to rebuild Jerusalem was issued in 457BC, we can then calculate the end of the 2,300 years as 22 October 1844. (L P Tolhurst – 'Ministry Magazine').

Here is a chart of the 2,300 days prophecy:

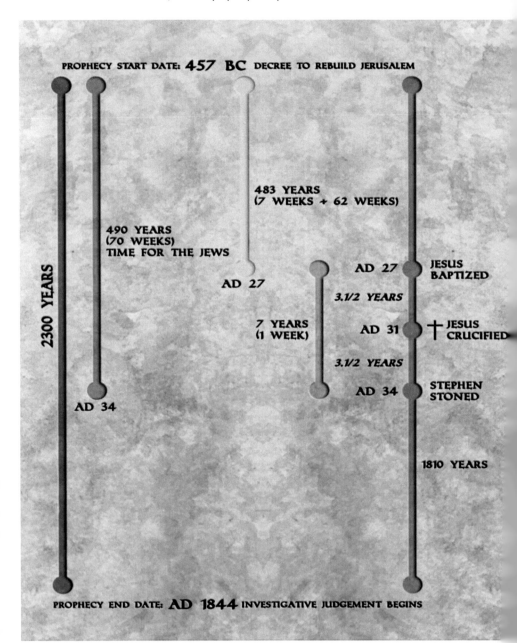

We will now consider the significance of the date 22 October 1844 for the Seventh-day Adventist Church.

In the early 1800s William Miller, a Baptist American Farmer, felt divinely led to study the prophecies of Daniel. He came to the 2,300 days prophecy and began to decipher the time lines as we have just done. Miller realised the sanctuary would be cleansed on 22 October 1844 and he began to preach this message to anyone who would listen.

Miller was not the only one to do this. Around the same time in Europe there were various Bible scholars who came to the same conclusion and began to preach the same message. This quickly developed into a worldwide movement.

At the time, there was a commonly held belief that the sanctuary, referred to in the prophecy, was the earth, and therefore the cleansing of the sanctuary was the destruction of the earth by fire and the creation of a new earth. In other words, that the cleansing of the sanctuary was the Second Coming or Advent of Jesus. Globally, around 300,000 believers were involved in this advent awakening. They called themselves Adventists.

The Adventists came from various religious denominations. The one belief they had in common was their certainty of the imminent second coming of Jesus.

William Miller learned of the cleansing of the sanctuary in 1819. Consequently, he believed the earth would exist for only another 25 years. Along with others, Miller preached the message in earnest and many thousands believed and joined the Adventists.

As 1844 drew near, people closed their businesses, ceased working their farms, left their employment and became evangelists. Finally, in October 1844 the

Adventists congregated in groups to await Jesus' return. Twenty-second of October dawned, some Adventists waited in great anticipation on hilltops, but the day passed and Jesus did not appear. It was a terrible disappointment, now known as the 'great disappointment'.

Revelation 10:8-10 prophesies this event.

Revelation 10:8 – An angel is shown holding an open scroll or *"little book which is open"* (KJV). As we have studied in the book of Daniel, Gabriel has been telling Daniel repeatedly that the visions given to him are not for his time. Then in Daniel 12:9 he is told the visions are to be *"closed up and sealed till the time of the end."* However, in Revelation 10 the little book in the angel's hand is open, which must indicate the time of the end has arrived. In 1819 William Miller, and others, were able to study and understand the prophecies of Daniel because the book was now open.

Revelation 10:9 – John the Revelator takes and eats the little book as instructed, and it is as sweet as honey in his mouth but bitter in his belly. In their study of the 2,300 days prophecy, the Adventists believed Jesus had revealed the date of His second coming. This knowledge was as sweet as honey, but when Jesus did not appear in 1844 the sweetness turned bitter, and the majority lost their faith. You can imagine Adventists telling their neighbours, families and friends they would not see them again after 22 October, and then having to face them on 23 October. They must have felt terribly humiliated. Some continued setting dates for the Second Advent and finally became discouraged when each date passed without incident. Large numbers returned to their original churches, and joined forces with those ridiculing the Adventists.

However, there was a small group of around 50 Adventists, who held on to their faith. Revelation 10:11 says the angel instructed that after the disappointment *"you must prophesy again before many peoples, and nations, and tongues, and kings."* (KJV). These Adventists went back to their Bibles to discover where they had gone wrong. They knew God had not forsaken them, and there was something for them to learn from this experience. They rechecked the time line of the 2,300 days prophecy and found it was sound. Therefore, the only thing they could have misinterpreted was the cleansing of the sanctuary.

As they studied, they were led to the book of Hebrews and found exactly what we learned in Daniel 8 – the sanctuary to be cleansed is the heavenly sanctuary, the one in which Jesus is presiding as our High Priest. They realised the cleansing of the sanctuary was the investigation of the record books of Jesus' professed followers. Once our books are examined, if our sins are confessed and so covered with the blood of Jesus, then God grants that our names be retained in the Book of Life, and we are pronounced a child of God. Our sins are then placed on the rightful person, the devil. And so, the sanctuary is cleansed of our sins.

The Adventists understood the reason for the great disappointment; God was preparing an end time church that trusted and served Him through the worst of experiences; a mature people who love God because they know Him, and whose faith could not be shaken. That is why the angel said *"you must prophesy again".* This end time church was given an end time message to preach to *"peoples, nations, languages, and kings."* (Revelation 10:11). And, they found the message in Revelation 14:6-12 which we now call 'The Three Angels' Messages'. This is the end time message for the end time people, and it is preached only by the end time church.

In Revelation 14:6,7 the first of these three messages calls people to worship the Creator of heaven and earth. This worship will be signified by adherence to the Ten Commandments, specifically, the fourth commandment which instructs us to keep the Sabbath day holy as a memorial of the creation of the earth in six literal days (see Exodus 20:8-11). In light of this, the Adventists began to keep the Seventh-day Sabbath, and in 1863 formerly adopted the name Seventh-day Adventists.

The First Angel's Message also warns that the Investigative Judgement is now taking place in heaven. We know this because of the 2,300 days prophecy. As the Adventists learned, 22 October 1844 was the date the throne of God was moved to the Most Holy Place of the heavenly temple (see Daniel 7:9), and Jesus Christ brought before Him (see Daniel 7:13) signifying the beginning of the Investigative Judgement (the judgement of God's people). Up until that time Jesus had been interceding for His people before His Father in the first compartment, or Holy Place, of the temple in heaven (see Hebrews 9:23-28).

22 October 1844 is a momentous date for it signifies the following:
- The beginning of the Investigative Judgement;
- The setting up of God's end time church;
- The preaching of the end time message to the world.

This Investigative Judgement will continue until every case is decided and judgement is given in favour of the saints (see Daniel 7:22). Then Jesus will come.

Revelation 14:8-12 details the Second and Third Angels' Messages. (These are fully explained in the companion book 'An Idiot's Guide to the Book of Revelation', chapter 14.)

The Seventh-day Adventist church is the only denomination that preaches the 2,300 days prophecy. The church was specifically set up by God to open this prophecy to the world, and proclaim the Three Angels' Messages in order to prepare the way for the second coming of Christ. Seventh-day Adventists do not claim to know the exact date of the Second Coming, but they do believe their God-given mission is an urgent one.

Footnote:

"So do not throw away your confidence; it will be richly rewarded. You need to persevere so that when you have done the will of God, you will receive what He has promised. For, 'in just a little while He who is coming will come and will not delay.'

"'But my righteous one will live by faith. And I take no pleasure in the one who shrinks back.' But we do not belong to those who shrink back and are destroyed, but to those who have faith and are saved." (Hebrews 10:35-39)

This text was one the Adventists held on to in 1844 following the great disappointment. Christians may get things wrong, but it is important they continue trusting that God is with them, and is still directing them. They must not *"shrink back"* even though they make mistakes. They may feel humiliated or ridiculed for the gospel's sake, but this is not the time to give up hope. At the very time when the situation appeared dark, dismal and desolate, a message of encouragement came from the Lord; *"You must prophesy again to many peoples, nations, languages and kings."* (Revelation 10:11 [KJV]). This message applies as much to us, as to the 19th century Adventists, for we are living in the time of the end. Jesus is soon to come, and the gospel must be preached.

Daniel Chapter Ten

THREE PRINCES

Based on Daniel 10:1-21

In Daniel 10 we meet a very perplexed Daniel.

Daniel 10:1-4 - Cyrus, king of Persia, is in the third year of his reign (535BC), and Daniel receives another revelation from God, which he cannot explain. All he knows is, the dream predicts a great war, and the message of the dream is true. In an effort to find the meaning of his dream, Daniel goes into mourning for three weeks: he uses no oils on his body, and abstains from choice meat and wine. Finally, on the twenty-fourth day of the first month, while Daniel is standing on the bank of the river Tigris, he receives a further vision in answer to his prayers.

Daniel 10:5-6 - Daniel sees an imposing figure, hovering above the river; a man dressed in linen, with a belt of the finest gold around His waist. His body shines like a precious Topaz stone, His face is like lightning, His eyes are like flaming torches, His arms and legs gleam like burnished bronze, and His voice sounds like a multitude. In Revelation 1:12-18 and Revelation 2:18 John, the Revelator is given similar visions of this man, who is identified as none other than Jesus.

Daniel 10:7-9 - It is interesting that although Daniel is not alone on the river bank, only he sees the vision of Jesus. However, those with Daniel, realise something supernatural is happening, and run away in terror. They are not able to stand in the presence of God, even though they cannot see Him. Revelation 6:15-17 tell of another time when men will be unable to stand in the presence of God. This happens at the Second Coming when those unprepared to meet Jesus, run to hide in caves and among rocks in order to get away from Him. Meeting with God is a disconcerting experience for mortals; both John and Daniel were faithful followers of Jesus, yet seeing Him in vision caused them both to lose consciousness.

Daniel is now alone. He gazes at Jesus but loses all his strength, his face turns deathly pale, and he is helpless. He hears Jesus speaking, but we are not told what He says, for it has all become too much for Daniel, and he faints.

Daniel 10:10-11 - The angel Gabriel, whom Daniel knows from his previous visions, comes to revive him. Daniel, although trembling, is able to stand up. Gabriel, once again, addresses Daniel as *"highly esteemed"*, and explains he has been sent to interpret the dream concerning the great war to come.

It must have been reassuring for Daniel to hear that he is still well thought of in heaven. For three weeks he has waited for an answer to his prayers. He may have felt this was due to some sin he had committed, or that God was displeased with him, but Gabriel's greeting puts his mind at rest. Gabriel will go on to explain the reason for the apparent delay. Those of us who have, at one time or another, wondered why God does not always answer our prayers immediately, can take comfort from Gabriel's explanation.

Daniel 10:12-14 - Gabriel makes it known that from the first day Daniel humbled himself before God to gain an understanding of his dream, God heard his prayer, and commissioned Gabriel to give its meaning. However, a spiritual battle to influence the mind of king Cyrus was in motion which hampered Gabriel's appointment with Daniel.

Gabriel had previously been sent to Cyrus to guide his decision making process. However, Gabriel's work was being blocked by someone he calls *"the prince of the Persian kingdom"* (Daniel 10:13). This 'prince' was endeavouring to control the king's thoughts, and Gabriel had to contend with him. As the prince was a negative influence on Cyrus, and strong enough to withstand Gabriel for three weeks, we can only conclude this prince was the devil himself, attempting to thwart God's plan. After a three week long battle to direct the actions of Cyrus, God decided enough was enough; Daniel must receive his answer. So a being named Michael came to Gabriel's aid and took on the struggle, enabling Gabriel to fly to Daniel to give him the interpretation of the dream that concerned the future of God's people.

Michael is undoubtedly a very powerful being. We have already learned Gabriel is the angel who stands in the presence of God. Michael, however, is the one called to help Gabriel when he is being opposed, and Gabriel refers to Him as *"one of the chief princes"* (Daniel 10:13). Therefore, Michael is no ordinary heavenly being, He is a chief prince. We are given a further clue to the identity of Michael in Daniel 10:21 where Gabriel, speaking to Daniel, calls Michael *"your prince"*. It is evident that Michael is Jesus. He is the one with the power to support Gabriel when obstructed by the devil. There are other instances in the Bible where Jesus uses the name Michael, such as Jude 1:9 and Revelation 12:7. He adopts this name when in fighting mode as Captain of the angelic host.

So now we can return to the question. Why does God not answer our prayers immediately? Daniel 10 gives insight into events taking place in the spiritual realm, which affect God's response time. It is clear God hears our prayers and desires to give us the answers we seek in accordance with His will. However, it could be that some related issue must be taken care of before we can receive the answer. Perhaps, in order for our petition to be granted, another person must be influenced for the good. The devil may be working on the mind of someone; tempting them to act in a way that will prevent our prayer from being answered as we wish. There are so many things we have no knowledge of; happenings behind the scenes that guide the actions of men. We cannot tell what is going on in the spiritual domain, and this may lead us to doubt God, but we need to trust Him. He knows what He is doing. We may not understand the way God works, but if we believe He loves and cares for us, we can feel assured that He is always seeking our good, and any apparent delay will be for our ultimate benefit.

Gabriel's explanation also assures us that God is so eager to answer our prayers, He will allow Jesus to take over an angel's battle in order to give us the response we so desperately need to hear.

The spiritual battles between good and evil angels for the hearts and minds of men, can take time, for God will not force the will of any human being. His angels speak to us, showing us the right path, but the devil and his angels are also present, prompting us to follow his evil and mischievous directives. We, who listen to both voices, have the power to choose whom we will obey.

Gabriel now attends to the matter of explaining Daniel's dream to him.

Daniel 10:15-19 – Again, Daniel suffers a physical reaction to all he is experiencing; he loses the power to speak and Gabriel once more has to revive him by touching his lips. Daniel's first words to Gabriel are an apology for his weakness and helplessness. He tells Gabriel *"....I can hardly breathe"* (Daniel 10:17). Gabriel then strengthens Daniel and reassures him he has no need to worry – he is highly esteemed by God. Gabriel encourages Daniel *"Be strong now, be strong"* (verse 19). Daniel feels strong again and is ready to hear the interpretation of his dream.

Daniel 10:20 - Gabriel warns Daniel that once he has revealed the dream's meaning, he must return to continue the fight against the devil, who is still seeking to control king Cyrus. He also reveals the prince of Greece (Alexander the Great) will shortly come to power. We know, from Daniel's earlier dreams, Alexander will follow the Medo-Persian kingdom, as ruler of the third world ruling empire in 331BC (see Daniel chapters 2,7 and 8).

Daniel 10:21 – Gabriel promises that before he returns to Cyrus, he will explain Daniel's dream. And, once again, Gabriel acknowledges Prince Michael (Jesus), who consistently supports him in his battles against the evil one and his minions.

Daniel 10 brings three princes to our attention:
- the prince of the Persian kingdom (the devil);
- the prince of Greece (Alexander the Great);
- Michael, your Prince (Jesus Christ), whom Gabriel proudly acknowledges as his supporter against Satan, the devil.

The war between Michael, our Prince, and Satan, the prince of the Persian kingdom, rages continually on planet earth. Invisible battles fought by supernatural beings affect our lives every day. The prince of the Persian kingdom has the power to influence our minds, but he cannot force us to commit evil. Each one of us is able to ask God for help when we feel an overwhelming urge to behave negatively. All we have learned in Daniel 10 confirms that God will despatch angels to fly to our aid at great speed and contend with this evil prince on our behalf. Their support enables us to gain victory over temptation, and choose to do right. If necessary, Jesus Himself will come to the rescue. What a wonderful promise!

In Chapter 11 we will examine the dream Gabriel interprets for Daniel.

Daniel Chapter Eleven - Daniel Chapter Twelve verse Four

THE KING OF THE SOUTH AND THE KING OF THE NORTH
(Gabriel gives a history lesson)

Based on Daniel 11:1-45 and Daniel 12:1-4

Daniel's dream, in Daniel chapter ten (which is still to be interpreted), was given around 535BC, two years after the first group of Jewish exiles returned to Jerusalem. The dream covers the period from the reign of the Persian Empire to the end of time. It is interesting that Daniel, who was taken from Jerusalem into captivity as a teenager, spent the rest of his life serving his captors. Despite his great concern for the freedom of his nation, he never returned to his homeland.

Daniel is now around 89 years old. Perhaps he considered himself too old to travel home. As predicted, the rebuilding of Jerusalem was completed in troublesome times (see Daniel 9:25), and could have been too much for the elderly Prophet to bear, but Daniel never lost focus. His attention was centred on Jerusalem. Therefore, he was consistently praying, fasting, and writing of the plight of the Jews. The dreams and visions he continued to receive concerned not only God's people of his time, but God's people down through the ages to the end of time. Daniel was determined to see the successful resettlement of his countrymen. God rewarded his persistence, and in addition, showed him the fate of spiritual Israel (the saved of all ages) in their attainment of the New Jerusalem (the heavenly city built by God).

Daniel 10:14 reminds us, the vision Daniel received is not for his time, but for the future. It extends to the latter days of earth's history, and concludes with the second coming of Jesus, just as his visions of Daniel 2 and Daniel 7.

In Daniel 11 Gabriel begins the interpretation of the dream received in Daniel chapter ten.

Daniel 11:1 – Gabriel continues his speech from the last verse of chapter ten, where he praises Michael (Jesus) for supporting him against the devil. Gabriel also reveals that in the first year of Darius, the Mede king, he was at the king's side to help and protect him. You will remember Darius was the king who threw Daniel into the lion's den (see Daniel 6). Darius ruled before Cyrus.

It is clear Gabriel has been guiding the actions of kings; aiding their rulership. God is interested in the world's political affairs. His angels protect those in power and influence them to do good in their leadership roles. Of course, God will not force anyone to follow His leading. Should a ruler decide to follow the promptings of the devil, he (or she) is able to exercise their free will to do so; and we have seen rulers throughout history who choose to rule through tyranny and injustice.

Here is the interpretation of Daniel's dream.

Daniel 11:2 – Gabriel explains that after Cyrus, three more Persian kings will rule, followed by a fourth who will be richer than his predecessors. This fourth king will gain power through his wealth, and stir up everyone against the Greek kingdom.

History tells us that after Cyrus, his son, Cambyses ruled (530BC-522BC), followed by Baridya (also known as False Smerdis) in 522BC, and then Darius the Great (not the Darius of chapter six) (522BC-486BC). The fourth Persian king after Cyrus was Xerxes, also known as Ahasuerus, (486BC-465BC). He did indeed stir up everyone against Greece, for he gathered an international army, numbering over 100,000 soldiers from 40 different countries. This vast military force attacked Greece, but lost battles both at the Bay of Salamis in 480BC and

Plataea in 479BC, which left the way open for a counterattack by Alexander the Great. ('Bible Study Guide - Daniel' 1987 page 141)

Daniel 11:3-4 – Alexander the Great described as *".. a mighty king..."* will arise, rule with great power and do as he pleases. And, as we already know from Daniel 7 and 8, Alexander was succeeded by his four military generals, who eliminated the king's descendants in 300BC. This is once again confirmed by Gabriel in verse 3, who adds that the dividing of the Greek kingdom will weaken it until it is finally given over to others.

Daniel 11:5-14 – We are now introduced to the conflicts between the king of the South and the king of the North. It is generally accepted that these conflicts describe the battles between the Ptolemies in the south and the Seleucids in the north; kingdoms arising out of the Greek Empire after the death of Alexander the Great.

"The Ptolemaic kingdom was founded in 305BC by Ptolemy I Soter, who declared himself Pharaoh of Egypt and created a powerful Hellenistic dynasty that ruled an area stretching from southern Syria to Cyrene and south to Nubia." (Wikipedia – 'The Ptolemaic kingdom').

"The Seleucid kingdom, (312BC–64BC), was an empire that at its greatest extent stretched from Thrace in Europe to the border of India. It was carved out of the remains of Alexander the Great's Macedonian empire by its founder, Seleucus I Nicator." (Britannica – 'The Seleucid kingdom')

Gabriel gives a comprehensive and detailed history lesson as he outlines various incidents in the reigns of the southern kingdom (Ptolemies) and the northern kingdom (Seleucids). For example, in verse 6 we are told of an alliance, made between the two kingdoms through marriage, that would break down due to treachery. This incident can be easily traced to the attempted alliance between the king of the South, Ptolemy Philadelphus of Egypt, and the king of the North, Antiochus Theos of Syria through the marriage of Ptolemy's daughter, Berenice, to Antiochus in 252BC. To enable the marriage, Antiochus had to divorce his first wife, Laodice (who was also his sister). Antiochus married Berenice, who bore him a son and heir. However, Antiochus then divorced Berenice and remarried Laodice, who took revenge on everyone by arranging the murders of Antiochus, Berenice, the attendants of Berenice, and Berenice's son. ('Bible Study Guide – Daniel' 1987 page 143)

Daniel 11:7-8 – Tell of the further revenge taken by Berenice's brother, who succeeded their father to the Ptolemic throne in 246BC. He attacked and defeated Syria and had Laodice put to death (Wikipedia). Gabriel also adds that Berenice's brother (the king of the South) will seize from Syria (the king of the North), the metal images of the Syrian gods, together with their silver and gold articles, and carry them off to Egypt. Then he will leave the king of the North alone for some years.

The battles between the southern and northern kingdoms continue through **verses 9-13**, as follows:

"Then the king of the North will invade the realm of the king of the South but will retreat to his own country. His sons will prepare for war and assemble a great army, which will sweep on like an irresistible flood and carry the battle as far as his fortress. Then the king of the South will march out in a rage and fight against the king of the North, who will raise a large army, but it will be defeated. When the army is carried off, the king of the South will be filled with pride and will slaughter many thousands, yet he will not remain triumphant. For the king of the North will muster another army, larger than the first; and after several years, he will advance with a huge army fully equipped."

Daniel 11:14 – Gabriel reveals that even the Jews will get caught up in rebelling against their invader, the king of the North. We know from Daniel chapters 2, 7 and 8 that the Roman Empire overthrew Greece in 168BC, and invaded Israel. Although the Jews rebelled against Rome through violent uprisings, such as those carried out by the Zealots in Jesus' time, each skirmish proved unsuccessful.

Daniel 11:15-16 – Tell us the king of the South is not able to withstand the power of Rome, which will even establish itself in Judea *"the Beautiful Land"*.

Daniel 11:17-19 - The Roman Empire will make frustrated efforts to set up alliances with the king of the South. It will continue its campaigns against the coastlands with varying success and then turn back to the fortresses of its own country, but the leader at that time will stumble, fall and be seen no more. This may refer to the defeat of Mark Antony at the battle of Actium (31BC) against Augustus, after which Mark Antony (and his lover Cleopatra) committed suicide. (Britannica)

Daniel 11:20 – We are told that in the kingdom of the North (Pagan Rome), the previous ruler will be succeeded by one who will *"send out a tax collector to maintain the royal splendour."* It is generally thought this refers to Caesar Augustus, the first Roman Emperor, who ordered a census of all Roman subjects for taxation purposes (see Luke 2:1 [KJV]). It was this decree that directed Joseph to take his heavily pregnant wife, Mary, to Bethlehem, and there Jesus was born (see Luke 2:3-7 [KJV]). Gabriel also predicts the manner of death of this Roman ruler. Gabriel says he will be destroyed in a few years, but not in anger or battle. History tells us Augustus ruled for 17 years and died at the age of 75, after a short illness.
(www.britannica.com/biography/augustus-roman-emperor)

Daniel 11:21 – The successor to Augustus will be *"a contemptable person"*. Undoubtedly, this is Tiberius Caesar who ruled after Augustus. Gabriel says this new ruler will not be accorded the honour of royalty. And indeed, Tiberius came to power after the death of Augustus, but did not allow the Roman Senate to proclaim him Emperor until a month after his reign began. Tiberius was a solitary and introverted character when he took the throne at the age of 54. At this time in his life he had learned to seek only his own satisfaction in cruel and perverse activities. (Britannica)

Daniel 11:22 - tells us this ruler will destroy the *"prince of the covenant"*. We can safely conclude the 'prince of the covenant' is Jesus, as in Daniel 9:27, we learned that the Messiah confirms the covenant with His people. It was during the reign of Tiberius that Jesus was crucified in AD31.

Daniel 11:23-28 - tell us about the exploits of this king of the North, who achieves more than his fathers or forefathers in distributing *"plunder, loot and wealth among his followers"* (verse 24). During his reign, Tiberius Caesar made twenty times more wealth for the empire than existed when he came to power. Under his rule, the power of Rome was made more financially secure than it had ever been. (Britannica)

The detail given by Gabriel of the exploits of this particular king of the North is impressive. Verse 27 tells of the kings of the North and South sitting across the same table with each other, as if in peace, but both their hearts are evil, and, they are lying to each other. Modern day rulers behave in a similar fashion. In 1985 President Ronald Reagan (USA) met with President Mikhail Gorbachev (Soviet Union) in the first summit conference of its kind. It appeared to be a massive step towards world peace. They hugged, kissed and smiled broadly for the media, however the underlying distrust and suspicion between these rulers of the most powerful countries in the world, sabotaged the process – sitting across a table but lying to each other. This model is repeated again and again in the world of politics.

Verse 28 warns, the king of the North's heart is set against the holy covenant. He takes action against it. The reign of Tiberius was not kind to the Jewish nation. At one point he exiled the entire Jewish community. (Britannica)

Daniel 11:29-39 – We see the king of the North, the Roman Empire, becoming more and more involved in religious activity, as Rome moves from its pagan phase to its papal phase:

- Verse 30 - Rome vents fury against the holy covenant and shows favour to those who forsake the covenant;
- Verse 31 – Rome desecrates the temple (AD70);
- Verse 31 – Papal Rome abolishes 'the daily'. Another reference to the transition from Pagan Rome to Papal Rome.

In Verse 31, we again see the *"abomination that causes desolation"*. We have seen this before in Daniel 7 and 9 as the little horn power (Papal Rome), in co-operation with the Roman State, sets up and enforces religious practices to replace the sacrifice of Jesus. These include the institution of Mass, and the usurping of the mediatory role of Jesus in heaven by appointing human priests to listen to confessions and absolve the confessor of sin. This, of course, is blasphemy; for only God can forgive sin (see Mark 2:7).

Verses 32-35 - tell us God's people will resist Rome's version of Christianity and, as a result, will be persecuted (see also Daniel 7:25). This, once again, refers to the Dark Ages (AD538-1798), a period of oppression that would last for *"Time, Times and half a Time"* (1,260 years).

Verse 36 - says the Papal power will be successful until its time of wrath is completed, for what has been determined must take place. Gabriel is confirming that although the Dark Ages will prove to be an abominable episode in earth's history, it must happen. Nevertheless, it is encouraging to note, that while millions were prepared to give their lives for the truth, their sacrifice was not unfruitful. The gospel of Jesus Christ spread more rapidly, and more people accepted Christianity during this time, than at any other period in history. The despicable activities carried out during the Dark Ages unveil the true character of the devil: his aim is to murder every person who gives his (or her) heart to Jesus. As Jesus revealed, the devil is truly a murderer (see John 8:44). The devil's objective to wipe the gospel out of existence has proved a monumental failure, for the more he incites the apostate church to execute those who follow Jesus, the more people take their stand for Him.

Verse 37 – The Papacy will exalt itself above all gods. This reminds us of the little horn power of Daniel 7:25 who acts as though he has authority over God Himself.

Verse 38 – tells us the Papal power will honour a god of fortresses with gold and silver, with precious stones and costly gifts. Certainly, the Papacy has honoured wealth throughout its existence. It remains the wealthiest church in the world.

Verse 39 – The Papal power will achieve great conquests, attacking the mightiest fortresses, even joining with countries who worship false gods. The Catholic Church forges alliances with nations that acknowledge its supremacy. It honours those nations, sets up rulers and distributes land to those able to purchase it.

Daniel 11:40–45 - The Papacy will conquer many nations. It will even invade the Beautiful Land. It will extend as far as Egypt and gain all its riches, with the Libyans and Nubians in submission. It will destroy and annihilate many.

From verse 40 onwards, the period under scrutiny is identified as the *"time of the end"*. This is the time when the Papacy engages in spiritual warfare in an attempt to bring all nations under its religious subjugation. We have been hearing about this final period in earth's history continually in the book of Daniel, and can identify its beginning as 1798. We will come back to this a little later. If we accept that the time of the end began in 1798, and the king of the

North at this time is the Roman Catholic Church, we should perhaps view the countries it is waring against as symbols of enemies of the Papacy during the time of the end. For example *"the Beautiful Land"* which in Daniel's time referred to Judea where God's people dwelt, now, during the time of the end, when the gospel of Jesus Christ is being preached to all nations, and all those who accept it are designated as spiritual Israel (see Galatians 3:29), we can interpret the Papacy's attack on 'the Beautiful Land' as the Roman Catholic's attack on God's people, wherever they are situated, during the period of the time of the end. Also, some Bible scholars compare the king of the North's extension of power over Egypt (Daniel 11:42) with the Roman Church's battle against Atheism during the French Revolution (1789-1799), when the Bible was burned in the streets, religion was banned, and Catholic priests sent to the guillotine together with the French nobility. However, the Roman Church was not destroyed. It survived, and became more powerful than before the revolution. (For more information on what the Bible has to say on the French Revolution see the companion to this book 'An Idiot's Guide to the Book of Revelation', chapter 11).

Certainly, Gabriel's discourse on the events of the time of the end reveals a time of great unrest. Mentioned, are Edom, Moab and Ammon, described as being delivered from the Papacy's hand. As these kingdoms no longer exist, we must view them as symbols. In ancient times, these nations opposed God, yet here we are told they are rescued from the Papacy's power. This indicates God will extend mercy to people who once opposed Him. The gospel of Jesus is universal. It is to be preached to *"every nation, tribe, language and people"* (Revelation 14:6). It gives all who live on earth, whether they be friends or enemies of God, the opportunity to receive salvation.

Verse 45 - says *"Yet he will come to his end and no-one will help him."* So we are promised this conquering king of the North (the Papacy) will come to its end during the *"time of the end"* (verse 40). This assurance confirms the predictions, made in Daniel 7:26 and 8:25, of the final destruction of the Papacy.

Finally, we come to the end of Daniel 11: certainly a challenging chapter, and one not fully understood, as it extends into our future. However, we can clearly see that it outlines, in great detail, the continual warring of the great nations of earth, from the reign of the Persian Empire to the end of time, and the effect of this on God's people. Once again, we see the emergence of the Roman Catholic Church, which wars against God's church, only to be destroyed at the second advent of Jesus.

Now we pass to Daniel 12 where we see Jesus' reaction to the attacks on His church.

Daniel 12:1-4 - continues in the period of the time of the end.

How can we be certain when the time of the end begins? To identify this period, let us return, for a moment, to Daniel chapter seven. In Daniel 7:25 we are introduced to the 1,260 years of Papal persecution of God's people (the Dark Ages; AD538–1798). Daniel 7:25,26 make it clear that the final destruction of the little horn power (the Papacy) takes place after the conclusion of the Dark Ages. In Daniel 7:27 and 11:40,45 we learn the Papacy's destruction will happen in the *"time of the end"*, then God's everlasting kingdom will be set up.

At the end of the Dark Ages, in 1798, Pope Pius V1 was taken into exile by General Berthier (Napoleon Bonaparte's General), and the great power of the Papacy was broken. This event, which Revelation 13:3 calls the fatal wounding of the Papacy, ushered in the time of the end. Gabriel has continually instructed Daniel that his visions are for the people living in the time of the end. And, as we have already learned in chapter 9, the book of Daniel became an open book to the studious Adventists in the early 19th century, shortly after the conclusion of the Dark Ages.

It is during the time of the end that Jesus will come back to earth to collect His people and set up His kingdom (see Daniel 7:27). In Matthew 24:29,30, in His explanation of the signs of His second coming, Jesus referred to the end of the Dark Ages and the beginning of the time of end when He predicted that immediately after the distress caused to His people during the Dark Ages, signs of His coming would be manifested in the sun, moon and stars. Then He will return. These signs actually took place on 19 May 1780 and 13 November 1833, when the sun turned black, the moon appeared blood red, and the stars fell from the sky in a magnificent shower of shooting meteors. All indicating the time of the end had begun. These events are recorded in:
- 'Webster's Unabridged Dictionary', edition of 1884, page 1604;
- 'Our First Century', R M Devens, page 32.

However, Revelation 13:3 also informs us the fatal wound of the Papacy will be healed. Therefore, although the Papacy was effectively abolished in 1798 this is not its final destruction prophesied in Daniel 7. It will be resurrected, and before its final demise when Jesus comes, the little horn will *"extend his power over many countries"* (Daniel 11:42). (For a full explanation of Revelation 13, and the modern revival of the Papacy, please see the companion book 'An Idiot's Guide to the Book of Revelation').

From the evidence shown above, we can confidently state that the time of the end began in 1798 following the end of the Dark Ages, and will extend until Jesus' second coming. Therefore, we are now living in the time of the end.

Daniel 12:1 - Gabriel says *"at that time";* (he is still referring to the time of the end), Michael, the great Prince (Jesus), will stand up.

Why does Jesus need to stand up? Because He has been sitting down. Hebrews 8:1,2 tell us Jesus has been sitting at the right hand of the Father, serving in the sanctuary as our High Priest and Mediator. When Jesus ascended to heaven (AD31), He sat down at the right hand of God His Father in triumph. At that time God's throne was situated in the Holy Place (or first compartment) of the heavenly sanctuary. Then, as we learned in Daniel 7:9, His throne was moved to the Most Holy Place (the second compartment) of the temple. And, Jesus also entered the Most Holy Place to again sit at the Father's right hand so that the Investigative Judgement could commence. These events happened on 22 October 1844 (see Daniel 7:13, Daniel 8:14). Since that time, Jesus has been pleading for the salvation of all those who have accepted His sacrifice, and claim His righteous character as their own.

Daniel 12:1 transports us to our future. Gabriel warns us, the time will come when Jesus will stand up because the Investigative Judgement has come to an end. The last professed Christian is judged, and now all God's true followers have their names written in the Book of Life. They are sealed by God (see Revelation 7:2,3), signifying they are designated as 'saved' and assured of eternal life.

Because they are sealed, God's people are equipped to go through a *"time of distress"*, also known as the *"time of trouble"* (Daniel 12:1 [KJV]) - the end time period of persecution for God's people (see Revelation 13:15-17). At that time, every person on earth will either bear the Seal of God or the Mark of the Beast. There will be only two groups at that time; each group has its mark. (For an explanation of these symbolic marks, please see the companion book 'An Idiot's Guide to the Book of Revelation', chapter 13).

Here is some good news. Daniel 12:1 promises that although God's people (whose names are written in the Book of Life) must endure a time of trouble, THEY WILL BE RESCUED.

Daniel 12:2 – tells how the saints will be delivered; Jesus will come. The advent of Jesus will herald the First Resurrection in which the righteous people who have died, will be raised from their graves, and ascend to meet Jesus in the air, together with the righteous people living on the earth (see 1 Thessalonians 4:13-18). These are the people who will gain eternal life.

In addition, at the Second Advent, another group, who do not follow Jesus, will also be resurrected. Matthew 26:63,64 and Revelation 1:7 refer to this special resurrection. The High Priest, Caiaphas, who was instrumental in engineering the death of Jesus, will witness His second coming, as will *"those who pierced Him"*, the soldiers who nailed Him to the cross.

The remaining masses, who have died without giving their lives to Jesus, will not come to life until the Second Resurrection. They will then face sentencing and final destruction (see Revelation 20). The Second Resurrection takes place at Jesus' Third Coming (see Revelation 20). Therefore, the High Priest and the soldiers will be brought to life in a special resurrection to witness Jesus return to earth as King of kings and Lord of lords. They come to life and experience *"shame and everlasting contempt"* (Daniel 12:2). Indeed, it will be a devastating realisation to learn they were responsible for crucifying the Son of God. (For an explanation of the events of Jesus' second and third advents, please see the companion book 'And Idiot's Guide to the Book of Revelation' chapter 20).

Daniel 12:3 - tells of people who come up in the First Resurrection. Gabriel calls them *"wise"*. Obviously, they have made the right decision. They have chosen to follow Jesus and are now rewarded with eternal life. They are also the ones who *"lead many to righteousness"*. Jesus made it clear that His followers will lead others to follow Him. In fact, it is the duty of each Christian to make known the good news of salvation to their family, friends and acquaintances – everyone within their sphere of influence (see Matthew 28:19,20).

Daniel 12:4 - Gabriel instructs Daniel to seal up the words of his book. He must write the visions down but they are not for his time. They are for our time – the time of the end, a time of frequent travel and increased knowledge. No-one can deny that knowledge has indeed increased during modern times. And, this is the age of incessant travel with ever multiplying modes of transport: mankind journeys to and fro, even into space.

Bible scholars believe the phrase in Daniel 12:4 *"Many will go here and there to increase knowledge"* also refers to the increased understanding of the book of Daniel in the modern age, and the global dissemination of its prophecies.

Being told to seal up the book must have been frustrating for Daniel. He spent over 70 years of his life writing a book he would never fully understand - a book for the future. For us living in the 21st century, the words of Gabriel have certainly been fulfilled; the visions of Daniel are no longer closed. We, the people of the time of the end, are now able to understand Daniel's prophecies.

As you read this book you are included in the fulfilment of Gabriel's instruction to Daniel.

Daniel Chapter Twelve (verses Five to Thirteen)

THE EPILOGUE

Based on Daniel 12:5-13

We have reached the epilogue in the interpretation of Daniel's final dream.

Now we know the dream's meaning, we can certainly appreciate Daniel's disquiet. He has viewed the detailed account of continuing wars occurring from his near future to the end of time. He was instructed to bear witness of these events, yet he would not live to see them take place.

His final dream begins with the closing stages of the Persian Empire, and takes us through events of the Greek Empire to its break-up. It continues with a comprehensive description of the disputes between the Ptolemies and Seleucids. Then charts the rise of the Pagan Roman Empire, later overtaken by Papal Rome. It culminates with the Catholic Church's war against God's people till, finally, they are rescued by the second coming of Jesus at the end of time, and the Papacy is destroyed.

Chapter twelve also serves as a fitting epilogue to the entire book of Daniel; as he is given special advice on what is expected of him, now he has received these revelations from God.

Daniel 12:5 - Remember, when Gabriel came to give the interpretation of the final dream, Daniel was standing on the bank of the Tigris river. He is still there. He sees two new figures, each standing on different sides of the river. They are conversing with the man dressed in linen, who is hovering above the river (in Daniel 10:5 we identified this *"man dressed in linen"* as Jesus). Jesus has returned to give the book's finale.   How wonderful that Jesus Himself completes Daniel's instruction.

Daniel 12:6 – One of the figures standing on the river bank asks Jesus *"How long will it be before these astonishing things are fulfilled?"* Good question! No doubt, this is exactly the question Daniel wanted to ask.   How long will God's people have to suffer at the hands of the king of the North (the Papacy)?

Daniel 12:7 – Jesus answers by raising both hands towards heaven, and swearing an oath in the name of God.   What better assurance that He is speaking the truth, the whole truth, and nothing but the truth.   The answer is *"It will be for a time, times and half a time.   When the power of the holy people has been finally broken, all these things will be completed."*

We should now be familiar with the time period *"time, times and half a time"*. We first came across it in Daniel 7:25. It is the 1,260 years of persecution for God's people - the Dark Ages (AD538 – 1798).   As millions of people were martyred during the Dark Ages, surely this signifies the power of the holy people being *"finally broken"*. However, Jesus emphasises here that the terrible oppression will come to an end.

Daniel 12:8 – Daniel is struggling to understand Jesus' answer, and little wonder; the fulfilment of His words lie over 2,000 years in Daniel's future. But he persists. He asks Jesus *"My Lord, what will the outcome of all this be?"*

Daniel 12:9 – Poor Daniel. He is once again told. 'Daniel you are not going to understand it.   It is not for your time'.

Daniel 12:10-12 – Nevertheless, Jesus goes on to give some extra hints and clues, as He frames the time of danger for the saints of God. This is additional information that confirms to us (rather than to Daniel) the calculation of the time periods already given.

Verse 10 – Jesus says *"Many will be purified, made spotless and refined......"* (or *"tried"* KJV). No doubt Jesus is referring to the many converts who will give their lives to Him, accept His righteousness as their own, and suffer sorely during the Dark Ages. *"......but the wicked will continue to be wicked. None of the wicked will understand, but those who are wise will understand."* Although many will surrender their hearts to Jesus, those who hear the gospel but refuse to repent, will continue in their wicked ways. Perhaps this also refers to the wicked Papal power that continually seeks to slay God's people. Jesus says the 'wicked' (those who do not follow Him), will never understand the prophecies given to Daniel. Only the 'wise' will receive the understanding. We have already learned from Daniel 12:1-3 that the 'wise' are those who follow Jesus, and are resurrected in the First Resurrection when He returns to earth.

It is interesting that in our time (the time of the end) the Bible, containing the book of Daniel, is readily available, and accessible. Yet Jesus says, those who refuse to follow Him will not understand it. Also, it is amazing that many still refer to the prophetic books of Daniel and Revelation as closed books; impossible to understand, when both Gabriel and Jesus Himself tell us they are specifically for our time. On the other hand, a quick search on YouTube will uncover a plethora of erroneous explanations of the prophetic books. Jesus promises that anyone who accepts Him as their Saviour will correctly understand the prophecies. Jesus truly is the answer; He is The Way, The Truth and The Life (John 14:6).

Verse 11 – Right at the close of the book, Jesus slips in a further two time prophecies to let us know we are on the right track. He says *".....from the time that the daily is abolished, and the abomination that causes desolation is set up, there will be 1,290 days."*

As Jesus has already warned, the dream's interpretation is not for Daniel's time, once again we must conclude the 1,290 days is prophetic time, and is thus governed by the prophetic time principle (one prophetic day = one literal year).

Therefore, 1,290 prophetic days equal 1,290 literal years. We now need to find a significant period of 1,290 years that begins with *"the daily"* being abolished. We have already come across the 'taking away of the daily' in Daniel 8:11 and Daniel 11:31. Both times this refers to the Papal power overtaking Pagan Rome, and instituting religious practices that deny the true sacrifice of Jesus. Also, in Daniel 9:27 we saw the *"abomination that causes desolation"* referring to the union of Political and Papal Rome, resulting in the oppression of God's faithful people. The *SDA Bible* Commentary, volume 4, page 881, interprets the 1,290 year period as follows:

"AD508 was the year in which Clovis, king of the Franks, stepped into the strategic position of the first civil power to join up with the rising Church of Rome. This laid the foundation for the centuries-long union of church and state, the abomination that causes desolation in Daniel 12:11. This was also the time in which many doctrines and practices that obscured Christ's high-priestly ministry became established in the church."

If AD508 is the start date of the 1,290 year period, then its end is 1798 – the beginning of the time of the end (508 + 1290 = 1798). And, this would make sense, for within this period lies the 1,260 years of the Dark Ages, the height of Papal supremacy, and the time when the Papacy practised and enforced a system of worship that negated Christ's sacrifice, and replaced His role as Mediator between God and His people, with the practice of confessing sins to Catholic priests.

Verse 12 – Jesus goes on to say *"Blessed is the one who waits for and reaches the end of the 1,335 days."* Again, we are dealing with prophetic time here.

151

There is nothing to suggest this is literal time; Jesus is still answering the same question. Therefore, the actual period is 1,335 literal years. If the 1,335 year period also begins at AD508, it would end in 1843, 45 years after the close of the 1,290 year period *(508 + 1335 = 1843)*.

This would mean all three time periods essentially cover the same era, with slight, but significant, differences in their start and end times.

Following this line of reasoning, the explanation would be that the 1,290 year period is a terrible time for God's people, signified by the uniting of Political and Papal Rome, which leads to 1,260 years of mass martyrdom. However, this time of oppression will end in 1798, and those living at that time will feel blessed, for they will experience the great religious revival culminating in the Advent movement of 1843.

1843 was the most exciting year for Adventists who believed in the imminent coming of Jesus. As far as they were concerned, they had only one more year to preach the Advent message, for they believed Jesus would return in 1844 (see chapter nine). More and more people were accepting the Advent truth and joining the movement. The eating of the little book referred to in Revelation 10 was still very sweet in their mouths (see Revelation 10:10).

Chart of the Daniel 12 timelines:

1,290 years   AD508 ⎯⎯⎯⎯⎯⟶1798
Political and Papal
Rome unite and
desecrate Biblical
truth.

1,260 years   AD538 ⎯⎯⎯⎯⟶1798
The Dark Ages:
Papal persecution
of God's people.

1,335 years   AD508 ⎯⎯⎯⎯⎯⎯⟶1843
God's people
who see the end
of this period will
be blessed.

Daniel 12:13 – Now Jesus comforts Daniel with a personal message. He tells him 'Continue the life you have been living Daniel. You will die, but that will not be the end for you. You will rise in the First Resurrection and be saved into My everlasting kingdom, where you will receive your eternal reward.' What a wonderful assurance. What better encouragement could Jesus give the bemused Daniel?

And, there we leave Daniel; a man highly favoured by God. He does not comprehend the visions given to him, but he has been promised he will gain eternal life. No doubt, throughout the years of eternity, all will be made clear to the great Patriarch.

And, what about us? The prophecies faithfully recorded by Daniel were written for our understanding. God has given us a message for our time. It tells of the rise and fall of earth's kingdoms; the great power that will war against God and His people; the Investigative Judgement presently taking place in heaven; the date when the time of the end begins; the message to be preached to the world before Jesus returns; and the identity of those who will inherit eternal life.

One thing is certain, God is the Author of these revelations. And, it is no coincidence that they have fallen into your hands. Now that you know what they mean, you have the opportunity to accept or reject them. You have all the information you need; you can choose to be on the side that wins.

TABLE OF PROPHETIC SYMBOLS IN THE BOOK OF DANIEL

SYMBOL	MEANING	BIBLE REFERENCE
Winds	Turmoil amongst nations	Jeremiah 25:31-33
Sea	Wicked people in tumult	Isaiah 57:20
Waters	Multitudes of people from different nations	Revelation 17:15
Beasts	Earthly kingdoms	Daniel 7:17
Eagle's Wings	Speedy and violent conquests	Habakkuk 1:6-8
Wings	Speed	Exodus 19:4
Multiple heads on beasts	Kings/Rulers	Revelation 17:9,10
Multiple horns on beasts	Kings/Rulers	Revelation 17:12
Time periods in prophecy	Day/Year principle (one prophetic day = one literal year)	Numbers 14:34 Ezekiel 4:6

Index

Theme	Chapter(s)	Page Numbers
M		
Man dressed in linen	10, 12	126, 148
Medo-Persia	2, 7, 8, 8:14, 10	16-18, 60, 62, 77, 92, 107, 131
Mene, Mene, Tekel, Parsin	5	41
Messiah, The	9, 11	114-117, 138
Michael	10, 11	129, 131, 134, 144
Miller, William	8, 9	95, 120-121
Most Holy Place, The	8:14, 9, 11	99, 102, 105, 123, 144
N		
Nebuchadnezzar, king	1, 2, 3, 4, 5, 6, 7, 8	1, 3, 5, 7, 10-14, 16-19, 21, 23, 25-28, 30-35, 37-40, 46, 53, 55, 58, 60, 66, 88, 92
O		
P		
Pagan Rome	7, 8, 8:14, 9, 11, 12	70, 94-96, 107, 109-110, 137, 139, 151

Theme	Chapter(s)	Page Numbers
P cont/d		
Papal power/Papacy, The	7, 8, 8:14, 11, 12	70, 75, 77-78, 84, 93-95, 104, 118, 139-143, 148-149, 150-151
Papal Rome	7, 8, 8:14, 9, 11, 12	70, 77, 92, 96, 107, 109-110, 139, 148, 151-152
Pope, The	7, 11	70, 74, 84, 143

Q

R

Ram	8, 8:14, 9	88-89, 92, 107, 110, 113
Roman Catholic Church, The	7, 8, 9, 11	78, 82, 84, 93, 96, 109, 141-142
Rome	2, 7, 8, 8:14, 9, 11, 12	16-18, 60, 66, 68, 70, 77, 81, 84, 92, 94-96, 107, 109-110, 137-139, 148, 151-153

S

Sabbath, The	7, 9	78-80, 109, 122
Scapegoat, The	8:14	102-103, 105

Theme	Chapter(s)	Page Numbers

Bibliography

- Babylonian Talmud: (Tractate Gitten 56b) (500BC).
- Devens RM (1877). Our First Century One Hundred Great Events. Springfield, USA:
  C A Nichols.
- Flick AC (2017). The Rise of the Mediaeval Church. California USA: Createspace Independent Publishing Platform.
- Geiermann P (1995). The Converts Catechism of Catholic Doctrine. Fort Oglethorpe, USA:
  Teach Services Inc Publishing.
- Herodotus (440BC). The Histories.
- Himes JV (1843). The Second Advent Manual. Boston USA:
  Joshua V Himes.
- Keenan S (2011). A Doctrinal Catechism (third Edition). South Carolina, USA:
  NABU Press.
- Keough GA (1987). Bible Study Guide – God and our Destiny. Nampa, USA: Pacific Press Publishing Association.
- Merriam-Webster (1884). Webster's Unabridged Dictionary. New York: Harper and Brothers.
- Nichol FD, Cottrell R, Neufeld DF, Neuffer J (1978). Seventh-Day Adventist Bible Commentary. Volume 4. Washington DC, USA:
  Review and Herald Publishing Association.
- Pfundl G (2004). Bible Study Guide – Daniel. Nampa, USA: Pacific Press Publishing Association.
- Toukam A (2016). The Sabbath - Catholic Virginian. To Tell You the Truth. North Carolina, USA:
  Lulu Press Inc.

- Veith WJ (2002). Truth Matters: Escaping the Labrinth of Error. British Columbia, Canada:
  Amazing Discoveries.
- von Harnack A (1987). What is Christianity (Texts in Modern Theology). Minneapolis, USA:
  Augsburg Fortress

Magazines:
- Tolhurst LP. Ministry Magazine. Establishing the date 457BC (April 1988).

Websites:
- www.ancienthistoryencyclopedia/titus
- www.britannica.com/topic/theseleucidkingdom
- www.britannica.com/biography/augustus-roman-emperor
- www.christianitytoday.com/ad70titusdestroysjerusalem
- www.nationalgeographic.com/culture/people/reference/constantine
- www.ushistory.org/alexanderthegreat
- Wikipedia – Death of Alexander the Great
- Wikipedia – Iron Age

Song:
- Cowper W (1773). God Moves in a Mysterious Way

General Reading:
- KJV – King James Version of the Bible
- NKJV – New King James Version of the Bible
- NIV – New International Version of the Bible
- White EG (2006). Early Writings. Washington DC, USA:
  Review and Herald Publishing Association.
- White EG (2012). Prophets and Kings. Nampa, USA:
  Pacific Press Publishing Association.

- White EG (2017). The Great Controversy between Christ and Satan. Nampa, USA:
  Pacific Press Publishing Association.